"Mountain, Moor and Loch"

GLEN FALLOCH.

"MOUNTAIN MOOR AND LOCH"

ILLUSTRATED BY

Pen and Pencil,

ON THE ROUTE OF THE

WEST HIGHLAND RAILWAY

WITH 230 ILLUSTRATIONS FROM ORIGINAL DRAWINGS MADE ON THE SPOT.

LONDON:
SIR JOSEPH CAUSTON & SONS.
1894.

Sir Joseph Causton & Sons
Printers & Publishers,
London.

DISTANCES.

—◆◆—

EDINBURGH TO FORT WILLIAM, 166 Miles.

—◆◆—

	Miles.
EDINBURGH TO GLASGOW (VIA FALKIRK) ...	47¼
GLASGOW (QUEEN ST.) TO CRAIGENDORAN ...	22¼
CRAIGENDORAN TO UPPER HELENSBURGH ...	2
UPPER HELENSBURGH TO ROW...	1¾
ROW TO SHANDON	2¾
SHANDON TO GARELOCH-HEAD	2⅓
GARELOCH-HEAD TO GLEN DOUGLAS	6¼
GLEN DOUGLAS TO ARROCHAR	4¼
ARROCHAR TO ARDLUI	8
ARDLUI TO CRIANLARICH...	8¾
CRIANLARICH TO TYNDRUM	5
TYNDRUM TO BRIDGE OF ORCHY	7½
BRIDGE OF ORCHY TO GORTAN...	8¾
GORTAN TO RANNOCH	7
RANNOCH TO CORROUR	7¼
CORROUR TO INVERLAIR	10
INVERLAIR TO ROY BRIDGE	5¾
ROY BRIDGE TO SPEAN BRIDGE	3¼
SPEAN BRIDGE TO FORT WILLIAM	9⅛

CORRIDOR CARRIAGE, WEST HIGHLAND RAILWAY.

SYNOPSIS.

—·◆·—

Linlithgow Palace—Glasgow—Queen Street Low Level Station—University and Scott Monument—Cathedral and George Square—The Clyde, its Docks and Shipping—The Exchange—Dunglass Castle and Bell's Monument, Bowling— Dumbarton Castle, the "Gibraltar of the Clyde"—Archway, St Patrick's— "Wallace's Seat"—Steamers at Bowling

LOCH LOMOND, NEAR ARDLUI.

THE WAY to THE HIGHLANDS
EAST COAST ROUTE

" I T'S a far cry to Lochaber," but in these days of luxurious locomotion the traveller is carried from London into the very heart of the Western Highlands with almost as little exertion as if he were going from the City to his

KING'S CROSS.

I

suburban home. Leaving late in the evening, he finds the long journey accomplished in the course of the night and early morning, and the through carriages of the great trunk lines are nowadays so comfortable that it is simply a case of being whisked along at lightning speed in bed or in an armchair. For those who prefer to travel by day, the beauty of the scenery, and the interest attaching to the places which are passed on the railway route to Edinburgh or to Glasgow, renders the trip a strong attraction in itself, although it cannot compete with the fascination of the Highland tour that has drawn them to the North, and which culminates after the two great Scottish cities are passed.

The EAST COAST route from the Metropolis to Scotland—393 miles to Edinburgh, whence it is a run of 47¼ miles to Glasgow, which lies at the door of the Western Highlands—links together three of the great railways; the Great Northern, from King's Cross to Doncaster; the North Eastern, from Doncaster to Berwick-on-Tweed; and the North British, from Berwick to Edinburgh and Glasgow. The ordinary carriages on this route are well nigh perfection in all the appliances for the comfort of the traveller, while corridor dining saloons and sleeping cars bring in the luxuries of railway transit. Through travellers may break their journey at Peterborough, Grantham, York, Durham, Newcastle, Berwick, or any station further north on the direct route.

On speeding from under the roof of King's Cross terminus, the northern suburbs are traversed, London being left behind when the Alexandra Palace is passed. Hatfield House, close to the line, is next noted. Soon after, there is seen on the left Knebworth House, the seat of Lord Lytton, and, passing through Hitchin and Biggleswade, we reach Huntingdon (58¾ miles from London). The famous fen country is now entered, and level plains are traversed, wrested by skilful drainage and tillage, from Whittlesea Mere. Peterborough (76¼ miles), which may be called the capital of the fens, presents a striking appearance, rising with its noble cathedral out of the flat lands around it. The cathedral is a magnificent specimen of Gothic architecture, and is recognised as being one of the most impressive ecclesiastical piles in Great Britain.

After a short stoppage, the train resumes its course, and at Essendine, Lincolnshire is entered. Soon after, the handsome tower of Caseby Church is seen on the right, and a little beyond we see Grimsthorpe Castle, the beautiful residence of Baroness Willoughby d'Eresby. Soon after passing Corby, and the church of Burton Coggles on the right, the highest point of the Great Northern system is reached, about 400 feet above the sea-level. We are now approaching Grantham (105¼ miles), which is the first stopping-place of the "Flying Scotchman" and the other famous East Coast expresses. The ordinary main line trains stop here for a few minutes. Grantham has a striking parish church in the Gothic style, with a crocketed spire 280 feet in height; but the town is mostly notable for the gigantic ironworks of Messrs. Richard Hornsby & Sons, which cover nearly seventeen acres and employ about 1,500 hands

Newark (120 miles), the next prominent point, is a town that has had a large part in the making of history. Its ancient castle has seen rough work since its foundations were laid by the Saxons, and in the civil war of the seventeenth century it was thrice besieged by the Roundheads, surrendering at last to the Scotch army of the Parliament. Leaving Newark behind, we pass through one of the finest fruit-growing districts in England, the country on both sides being almost continuous orchards. Passing through Retford (138½ miles), we come to Scrooby, a famous meeting-place of the "Pilgrim Fathers" before they sought asylum in America. At Doncaster (156 miles)—a name familiar to everybody—attention is attracted by the fine parish church (a splendid example of pointed architecture, but dating only from the middle of the present century), with a tower 170 feet in height dominating the town. Soon after leaving Doncaster, Shaftholm Junction is passed, where the train changes from the metals of the Great Northern to those of the North Eastern. Then Selby is reached, and the Ouse is crossed.

York (188 miles from London) is the first point at which there is a stoppage of any duration, an interval of twenty minutes for refreshment being given to the day trains. It is one of the most interesting cities in the kingdom, with

3

its wonderful Minster and its ancient walls · The walls date from 1280, when they were built by Edward the First, and the city gates stand now as then, although more than six centuries have passed over them. The beginning of the glorious Minster was early in the seventh century, but the present edifice is said to have been commenced in 1171. After leaving York, we pass Thirsk Junction (210½ miles) and Northallerton Junction (218 miles), the name of the latter reminding us that there the "Battle of the Standard" was fought in 1138, when the Scots were defeated by the English army under the Archbishop of York. Crossing the Tees, we enter Darlington (233 miles), "the cradle of English railways," and a centre of the worsted industry. It was from Darlington to Stockton, a few miles distant to the northeast, that in 1825 George Stephenson constructed the first railway ever opened for passenger traffic.

We are now in the great iron and coal district, but a pleasant change from the industrial character of this part of the country is afforded by the city of Durham (254 miles), with its noble cathedral towering on a height that rises from the waters of the Wear. The architecture is of the Norman period, and the lantern tower, 214 feet in height, dates from the thirteenth century. The town is also notable for its fine Castle, now forming part of the University.

Gateshead (267½ miles) is the next town of importance, lying on the southern bank of the Tyne, facing Newcastle. Like the latter, it is a centre for collieries, iron works, and other grimy industrial necessities, and although it is not beautiful, it is decidedly interesting. The Tyne is crossed by Robert Stephenson's mighty High Level Bridge (1,337 feet in length and 112 above the water), which cost nearly half a million to build. Newcastle (268½ miles) has many claims to interest— especially the remains of the eleventh-century Castle,—whence the name is derived, but they are all dwarfed by the importance of the town as a coaling centre.

Leaving Newcastle behind, the coal districts are gradually lost to view, and by the time Morpeth (285 miles) is reached, the scenery is charming again. Soon glimpses of the sea may be had, and presently Bamborough Castle is seen on a com-

4

manding rock, four miles from the shore, while on a clear day may be detected the Farne Islands, where Grace Darling performed her heroic rescue. Skirting the cliffs, we reach the Tweed, the boundary between England and Scotland, which is crossed by a bridge of twenty-eight arches, 2,160 feet in length and 126 feet above the water. The opening of this bridge, in 1850, by the Queen, was aptly described as "the last act of the Union."

NORTH BRITISH WAVERLEY STATION, EDINBURGH.

Berwick-upon-Tweed (335½ miles) is in a curious position, inasmuch as it is a part of neither England nor Scotland, but is a separate county and free town to itself. In the olden days the Scots and the English were continually contending for its possession, and its sixteenth century ramparts and gates are still in good preservation. At Berwick-upon-Tweed, where there is a stoppage of a few minutes, the North Eastern Railway ends and the North British begins. The line continues to follow the curve of the coast, and skirting Halidon Hill on the left, the train enters Scotland at Lamberton, at one time an east coast Gretna Green. Thence the first important point is the ancient town of Dunbar (364 miles), where Cromwell gained his great victory over the Scottish Army in 1650. Opposite Dunbar may be seen towering out of the sea to a height of over 400 feet, the Bass Rock, whereon an old State prison used to stand. Following the Firth of Forth, and looking across to Fife, we pass through Prestonpans, where Prince Charlie in the '45 defeated Sir John Cope; then comes Portobello, which serves as a seaside suburb for Edinburgh. Three miles further and the Scottish capital itself is entered (393 miles from King's Cross), the sight of Arthur's Seat rising over the city, bringing home to the traveller the agreeable fact that he has really reached the land of hills. The short run from Edinburgh to Glasgow, and thence to the Western Highlands, is described in a subsequent section.

A BIT OF THE OLD TOWN,
EDINBURGH.

THE MIDLAND ROUTE

Another route is by the Midland Railway, *viâ* Leeds, Settle and Carlisle, and thence to Edinburgh, Glasgow, and all places in the North, by the North British.

On leaving St. Pancras, a short run of eighteen miles brings us to the cathedral city of St. Albans, whence the great Lord Bacon took his title, and where he lies buried. Passing through Chiltern Green and the "Chiltern Hundreds," so

ST. PANCRAS.

A

familiar in Parliamentary life, we reach Bedford (49¾ miles), with Elstow close by, associated with the name of John Bunyan. Wellingborough follows, a town with the ruins of Croyland Abbey near, and presently Kettering (72¼ miles) is reached, both towns centres of the Northamptonshire boot and shoe industry. It was in Kettering that the first missionary meeting was held in England. Leicester (99¼ miles), the focus of a great wool-growing country, is the next noteworthy point, an ancient town celebrated for many things, but perhaps most of all for the introduction of the stocking-frame. Passing through Loughborough (111¾ miles), Trent (120 miles), and Ilkeston (126½ miles), we come to Chesterfield (146¼ miles), where attention is riveted by the church of St. Mary and All Saints on the hillside, with an extraordinary leaning spire, curiously twisted in a most singular fashion. We are now in the heart of the Midland coal and iron fields In the church of the Holy Trinity at Chesterfield lie the remains of George Stephenson, to whom the neighbourhood owes so much of its prosperity. At Ilkeston this route is joined by trains going northwards *via* Kettering by way of Melton Mowbray and Nottingham.

Sheffield (158½ miles), the renowned seat of the cutlery and implement trades, is the next town of importance, and although placed amid beautiful surroundings, it would be difficult to imagine a more unlovely town, it being wholly devoted to that metal working which has made the name of Sheffield steel known the world over. To turn the eye from the mass of smoking chimneys that represents Sheffield, to the environments of the city is one of the most abrupt contrasts afforded anywhere in Great Britain. Five rivers converge where Sheffield has been built, and from their banks rise well-wooded hills, forming a most picturesque setting for such a "black diamond." Leeds (198 miles), the centre of the woollen trade, is the next considerable city, and close by, on the banks of the Aire to the right, a view is obtained of the beautiful ruins of Kirkstall Abbey. A little further on we pass through the model village of Saltaire, built by Sir Titus Salt, the philanthropist and manufacturer, for the use of his workpeople.

From Settle (236¾ miles) onwards to Carlisle the scenery is magnificent, the railway threading for seventy-two miles a mountainous district presenting almost insurmountable engineering difficulties in the construction of the road in 1869. Settle itself is a pleasant little market town surrounded by romantic scenery, some of the most picturesque scenes in the West Riding being within easy reach. We proceed onwards through Yorkshire, Westmoreland and Cumberland, piercing the Pennine range, and winding in and out amongst its numerous spurs, through country so rugged that the construction of the seventy-two miles of railway involved an expenditure of over three millions, while seven years were spent in the task, the principal engineering features being nineteen viaducts and thirteen tunnels, with innumerable deep cuttings and high embankments

Proceeding up Ribblesdale, we note on the right Pen-y-Ghent, a fell 2,273 feet in height, while a few miles further north rises Ingleborough (2,374 feet) on the left, and on the right Whernside (2,414 feet) Batty Moss is crossed by a gigantic viaduct, 1,328 feet in length, and 165 feet above its foundations ; and Blea Moor is traversed by a tunnel 2,640 yards in length and 500 feet below the surface. From the Dent Head viaduct a fine view is obtained of lovely Dentdale on the left, and, later, Garsdale is seen on the same side. North of Hawes Junction, Aisgill Moor is crossed, standing 1,167 feet above sea level, and Westmoreland is entered between Wild Boar Fell (2,323 feet) on the left and Shunnor Fell (2,346 feet) on the right The way is now along the romantic Eden Valley, and after passing Appleby (277¾ miles) and leaving behind, on the right, Cross Fell (2,901 feet), the highest of the Pennine Hills, we reach Carlisle (308 miles).

Here we are on the borders of Scotland, and, owing to its situation, Carlisle has seen much of war in the days when the English and the Scots were two nations. It was besieged by the Parliamentary Army during the Civil War, and had to surrender, and it is associated in the memory with the march into England of Prince Charlie in the '45. Picturesqueness is given to the town by the cathedral and the castle on the high ground overlooking the River Eden.

If Edinburgh be taken as the starting point for the Western Highlands, the passenger traverses the land of Scott. Through Eskdale we go, passing Netherby Hall, the scene of the ballad of "Young Lochinvar," cross the line of the Cheviot Hills and next the River Teviot, reaching Hawick (353½ miles), an important seat of the Scotch tweed manufacture. Skirting the Tweed valley, which lies on the right, we pass close to the ruins of Melrose Abbey. Crossing the Tweed, the Gala Water is followed to Galashiels, another centre for tweeds and tartans, and presently Edinburgh is reached—406½ miles from London.

FISH-WIVES, EDINBURGH

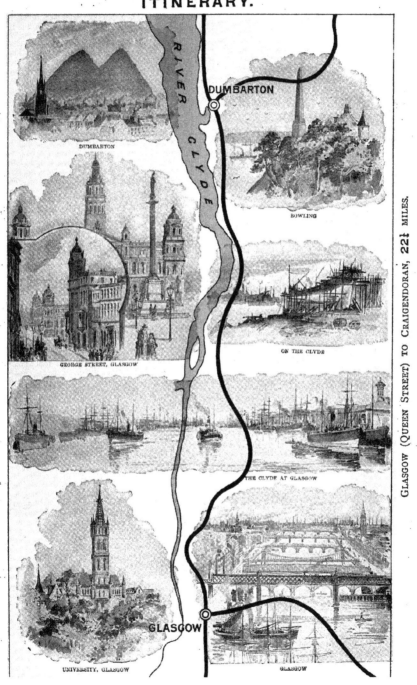

DUMBARTON

BOWLING

DUMBARTON

ON THE CLYDE

GEORGE STREET, GLASGOW

THE CLYDE AT GLASGOW

GLASGOW

UNIVERSITY, GLASGOW

GLASGOW

RIVER CLYDE

Glasgow (Queen Street) to Craigendoran, 22¼ miles.

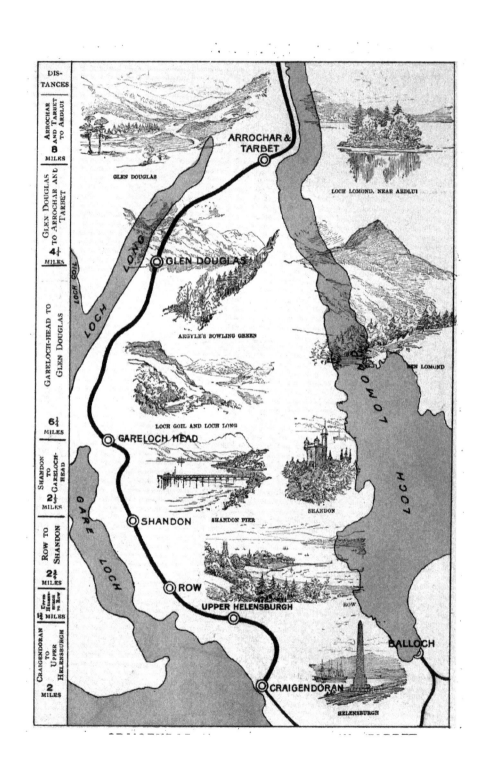

ARROCHAR & TARBET

GLEN DOUGLAS

LOCH LOMOND, NEAR ARDLUI

LOCH GOIL

LOCH LONG

GLEN DOUGLAS

ARGYLE'S BOWLING GREEN

BEN LOMOND

LOCH LOMOND

GARELOCH HEAD

LOCH GOIL AND LOCH LONG

GARE LOCH

SHANDON

SHANDON PIER

SHANDON

ROW

UPPER HELENSBURGH

ROW

BALLOCH

CRAIGENDORAN

HELENSBURGH

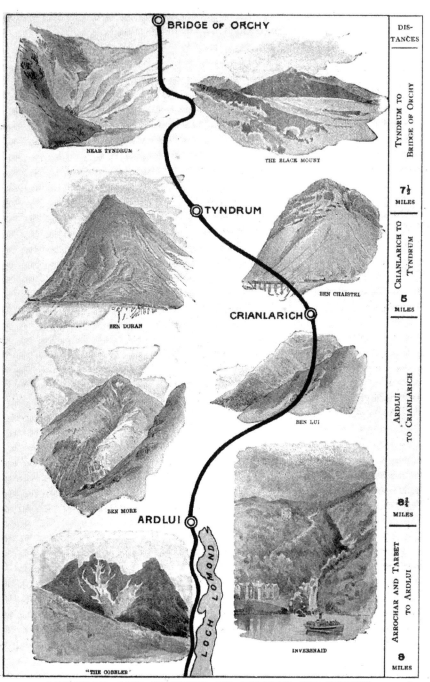

BRIDGE of ORCHY

NEAR TYNDRUM

THE BLACK MOUNT

TYNDRUM

BEN DORAN

BEN CHAISTEL

CRIANLARICH

BEN LUI

BEN MORE

ARDLUI

LOCH LOMOND

"THE COBBLER"

INVERSNAID

DISTANCES

TYNDRUM TO BRIDGE OF ORCHY

7½ MILES

CRIANLARICH TO TYNDRUM

5 MILES

ARDLUI TO CRIANLARICH

8¼ MILES

ARROCHAR AND TARBET TO ARDLUI

8 MILES

ARROCHAR AND TARBET TO BRIDGE OF ORCHY.

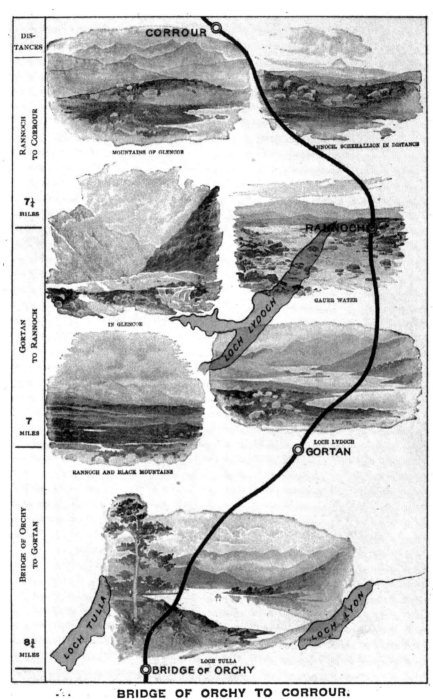

CORROUR

RANNOCH TO CORROUR

MOUNTAINS OF GLENCOR

RANNOCH, SCHEHALLION IN DISTANCE

7½ MILES

RANNOCH

LOCH LYDOCH

GAUER WATER

IN GLENCOE

GORTAN TO RANNOCH

7 MILES

RANNOCH AND BLACK MOUNTAINS

LOCH LYDOCH
GORTAN

BRIDGE OF ORCHY TO GORTAN

LOCH TULLA

LOCH LYON

8¼ MILES

LOCH TULLA
BRIDGE OF ORCHY

BRIDGE OF ORCHY TO CORROUR.

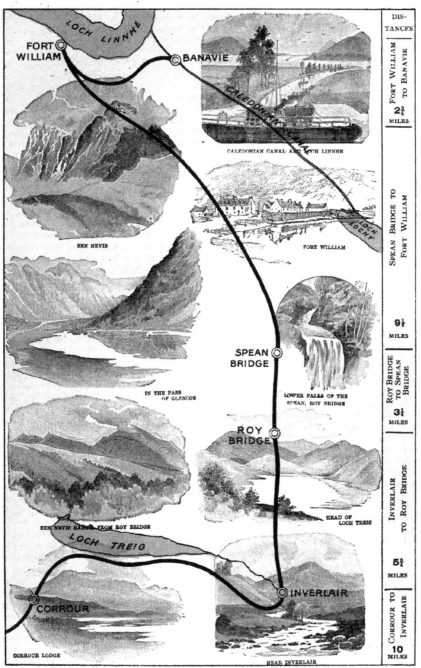

FORT WILLIAM
LOCH LINNHE
BANAVIE
CALEDONIAN CANAL
LOCH LOCHY
CALEDONIAN CANAL AND LOCH LINNHE
FORT WILLIAM
BEN NEVIS
SPEAN BRIDGE
LOWER FALLS OF THE SPEAN, ROY BRIDGE
IN THE PASS OF GLENCOE
ROY BRIDGE
HEAD OF LOCH TREIG
BEN NEVIS RANGE FROM ROY BRIDGE
LOCH TREIG
INVERLAIR
CORROUR
CORROUR LODGE
NEAR INVERLAIR

DIS-TANCES
FORT WILLIAM TO BANAVIE
2¼ MILES
SPEAN BRIDGE TO FORT WILLIAM
9½ MILES
ROY BRIDGE TO SPEAN BRIDGE
3¼ MILES
INVERLAIR TO ROY BRIDGE
5¼ MILES
CORROUR TO INVERLAIR
10 MILES

CORROUR TO FORT WILLIAM AND BANAVIE.
SECTION 5

A Bird's Eye View

BEN A CHAISTEL AT AUCH.

I F you look at the map of Scotland you will see that the country on the West, is simply torn to tatters by lochs, either inland sheets of fresh water or far-reaching arms of the Atlantic ; while the land thus broken up is black with hill-shading wherever the streaks and patches of blue leave a tract of dry land big enough to build a mountain upon. Argyllshire, Inverness-shire, Perthshire and Dumbartonshire, as presented by the maker of maps, may be compared to the colours of some fighting regiment, after half a century of arduous campaigning, blackened by powder and rent by bullet. This is putting it poetically, but a more prosaic comparison would be to say that these West Highlands on the map are like a cabbage-leaf devoured by caterpillars.

Such a wild and picturesque district is a very Paradise for the tourist, but hitherto this "Land of Mountain, Moor and Loch" has been remarkably difficult of access. It is traversed diagonally by the chain of lochs that form the Caledonian Canal, cutting through Argyllshire and Inverness-shire from the Island of Mull to the Moray Firth, like the straight slash of a knife, and the traveller has been enabled to skirt these rugged shires by steamer, while he has also been able to penetrate far into Argyll and Dumbarton by the great southern lochs ; but where the

paddle-wheel ceased to revolve there has been no loco-
motive to take up the running. From the stopping-points
of the steamers, there have been a few coach routes, but these
have covered only an infinitesimal part of this marvellously
beautiful country, and hitherto the land west of the Grampians, from Lochaber, south to the sea, has been left almost
alone to the pedestrian or cyclist of untiring muscle. Hitherto
one railway alone has intruded amongst these glorious glens,
these frowning peaks and gleaming lochs—the line that runs
from Killin in Perthshire, almost due west, bisecting the

GARELOCH.

Argyllshire Highlands. But nearly all the passengers by this
route have been making straight for the terminus at Oban,
and in the short run after the Grampians are crossed, have
had nothing more than a glimpse of the scenery now
completely opened up from South to North.

The West Highland Railway, now completed, breaks
fresh ground from start to finish of its hundred-mile run;
carrying the traveller through what is, perhaps, the most
sublime and characteristic portion of Scotland. Taking up
at Helensburgh, which lies at the mouth of the Gareloch,
an uncompleted end of the North British Railway, it

winds northwards along the base of the Grampians to Inverlair, whence it strikes westwards through Lochaber to Fort William on Loch Linnhe, which with a branch to Banavie, makes connection with the Caledonian Canal, and brings within the reach of the traveller the most tempting possibilities in the way of circular tours. Now in Dumbartonshire, now in Perthshire, now in Argyllshire, now in Perthshire again, now in Inverness-shire, it never for one moment meets the prosaic: the panorama of landscape that

LOCH KATRINE.

passes before the carriage windows changing almost every minute, into more and more bewitching visions of infinite variety. As the Irish navvy engaged on the construction of the line observed, "Sure, it's the most amphibious country ever seen by the naked eye"—so many sheets of deep blue water break upon the sight as the train sweeps round each curve, that to the non-engineering traveller, it seems as if a new Caledonian Canal might have been constructed almost as easily as a railway; while the hills are piled on each other in such multitudinous profusion that the opening out of each new vista of towering peaks fairly intoxicates an artist with delight.

The scenery may be divided roughly into four sections. From Helensburgh to Ardlui the line hugs in succession the shores of three great lochs—Gareloch, Loch Long, and Loch Lomond—which cleave their way through grand mountain barriers; from Ardlui to Gortan, it threads its course along a bewildering maze of stupendous crags; from Gortan to Rannoch, it traverses the great Moor of Rannoch, which has no parallel in Britain; and from Rannoch to Fort William it passes through a country that combines all the features of the previous stretches, loch, moor and glen, overhung· by vast eminences scattered over the land with lavish prodigality— Ben Lomond, Ben Ime, Ben Vane, Ben Voirlich, Ben More, Ben Doran, and a phalanx of other mountains, culminating in mighty Ben Nevis   Never was there a railway that less disfigured the country through which it passed.   Like a mere scratch on the mountain slopes, it glides from valley to valley, unobtrusive as a sheep path, and not even John Ruskin would regard it as a desecration of the Highland solitudes.   Along the course of this West Highland Railway little evidence of cultivation meets the eye of the super- ficial observer; and yet many of the best sheep farms of Scotland—in some instances feeding not less than 20,000 head of the finest black-faced sheep of the country—are found on the lands traversed by it.   It is a land of sport, the home of the deer, the grouse and the white hare, while the streams abound with trout, and those who know it will cease to wonder why the old clansmen who inhabited those bare yet beautiful glens sought so often and so successfully to make the cattle of the Lowlands their own.   Up to Ardlui, houses are far apart, but still one feels that the country is inhabited; north of that place houses are few, and when a dwelling-place appears it is generally a low thatched hut, and you have to look twice before asserting dogmatically which is the house and which is the haystack.

If ever there was a railway which was so evidently a railway for the tourist and holiday-seeker, it is the West Highland.   Manufactures there are none, but the railway will give to agriculture and farming, facilities hitherto unknown, and there will, without doubt, be an increased traffic in sheep and cattle, which will find a new outlet to the South from the districts converging on Spean Bridge and at other points of the line. Industries will doubtless grow, now that the railway is opened, but goods traffic will require some years to develop, although the well-known "Long John" whiskies of Fort William will contribute something. It opens up a world hitherto known only to the sportsman and to the comparative few who, with abundant leisure and means, could penetrate the magnificent country through which it passes. Beyond this, the extensive country which is brought within

STRATHFILLAN.

easy access of the commercial metropolis of Scotland will be developed by the industry and enterprise, characteristic of the industrious and intelligent community which has given Glasgow so prominent a place among the cities of the Empire. Not only does it throw open a new land of promise, as we have shown, but it will shorten by upwards of an hour the journey between Edinburgh or Glasgow and Oban —a watering-place that requires no introduction to popular favour. Along the line, coach roads strike off to right

and left, taking the traveller through the many interesting
districts into which the railway runs—the "Rob Roy" country,
the "Lady of the Lake" country, and the ever famous
Glencoe—making connection with steamboat services on the
lochs, and transporting him whither he will, by land or by
water, over this happy hunting ground of the tourist. Now
that the bridle track and sheep path have been supplemented
by the iron-way, in such an embarrassment of alluring alternatives, the difficulty is not to find a route, but to select one,
for the West Highland Railway emphatically forms perhaps
the greatest of the great "show-routes" of Britain.

LOCH EARN.

The Approaches

TOLBOOTH,
— EDINBURGH.

THE traveller, having arrived in Scotland, finds two centres from which the West Highland Railway may be reached—viz., Edinburgh and Glasgow—and, starting from the former, he passes through the latter, thus seeing both the principal cities of Scotland. The approach from both points is by the North British Railway, under whose auspices the West Highland has been constructed, the distance between Edinburgh and Glasgow being covered in about an hour and a quarter.

No tourist from the South can afford to dispense with a visit to Edinburgh, the capital of Scotland, and one of the most picturesque and polished cities in Europe. Since Stuart, author of *The Antiquities of Greece*, dubbed it the "Modern Athens," the phrase has become hackneyed; but the first glance at Edinburgh, from almost any point of view, will show the stranger that this description, though rendered trite by repetition, is happily selected. On three hills the city is built, overlooking the waters of the Firth of Forth, which lie two miles distant to the north-east. Around the city are grouped commanding eminences, Salisbury

SCOTT MONUMENT, EDINBURGH.

Crags and Arthur's Seat towering up in the east from the plain on which stands old Holyrood Palace; while to the south-west lie the Pentland,

PRINCES STREET, EDINBURGH.

Braid, and Blackford Hills, and to the north-west the high ground of Corstorphine. Over the three ridges on which it is placed, the city undulates with a fine but yet harmonious irregularity that renders "the long unlovely street" of other towns the exception instead of the rule. The grey Castle, on its commanding rock, overlooks the quaint "Old Town" peopled with the ghosts

EDINBURGH FROM CALTON HILL.

KNOX'S HOUSE,
EDINBURGH.

ST.
ANTHONY'S
CHAPEL
EDINBURGH.

of Scottish history; and the Calton Hill, crowned with imposing monuments, looks down on the "New Town," beautiful in architecture generally, and especially striking in the view along Princes Street, flanked on the left by public gardens—filling the ravine, known of old as the "Lang Dike," and more

HOLYROOD, FROM CALTON HILL.

recently as the "North Loch," and on the right by its parallel lines of fine streets, broken with others intersecting, giving glimpses of the Firth—glittering in summer sunshine—beyond, making it undoubtedly the handsomest thoroughfare in the three kingdoms.

As the day darkens into night a most imposing and singular sight is the display of lights from the irregular levels of the buildings of the "Old Town," as seen from Princes Street, giving one the idea of some general illumination rather than the ordinary every night aspect of the city.

Leaving Waverley Station for Glasgow, the train passes under the shadow of the Castle Rock, past the Princes Street

EDINBURGH CASTLE: WEST GATE.

Gardens, and is almost immediately in the country, skirting Corstorphine Hill on the right, and the Pentland Hills on the left. There is no grandeur in the scenery, but it is

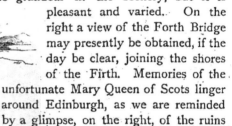

A GLIMPSE OF THE FORTH BRIDGE FROM CALTON HILL.

pleasant and varied. On the right a view of the Forth Bridge may presently be obtained, if the day be clear, joining the shores of the Firth. Memories of the unfortunate Mary Queen of Scots linger around Edinburgh, as we are reminded by a glimpse, on the right, of the ruins of Niddrie Castle, the residence of the Setons in those days. Readers may remember the song supposed to have been sung by one of the Queen's Maries on the day of her leaving Scotland :—

"Last night there were four
    Maries ;
    To-night there will be but
    three !
There was Mary Beaton, and
    Mary Seton,
    And Mary Carmichael —
    and me."

Mary Seton was one of Mary Stuart's dearest friends, and to Niddrie

QUEEN MARY'S BATH, EDINBURGH

Castle the Queen fled straight-
way, on her escape from Loch-
leven Castle. Another historical
resting - place is soon passed —
Winchburgh — where Edward the
Second first drew bridle after his
crushing defeat by Robert the Bruce, at Bannockburn—about
twenty miles distant as the crow flies.

The next point of interest is Linlithgow, where we see,

WEST PRINCES STREET GARDENS, EDINBURGH

on the right, the fine ruins of the Palace, on an eminence overlooking the lake. Here Mary Queen of Scots was born in 1542; and in the vaults James the Third sought refuge from assassination. In St.

LINLITHGOW PALACE.

Michael's Church, near by, the finest of the collegiate buildings of Scotland, and closely associated with the history of the Stuart Kings, James the Fourth saw in the aisle by night the vision that warned him against the coming fate of Flodden, as related under Sir David Lindesay's tale in "Marmion." In the streets of the town the Regent Murray was shot from an upper casement, as he rode along, by Hamilton of Bothwellhaugh. Falkirk next attracts attention on account of the great ironworks there —conspicuously the Carron Company on the right, the first in Scotland to start iron-

QUEEN STREET LOW LEVEL STATION, GLASGOW.

smelting on a large scale. Falkirk is not picturesque by day, but by night, when the blast furnaces are blazing in the darkness, it might be a scene from "Paradise Lost," or the "Inferno." From this point there is a fine view over the winding

GLASGOW UNIVERSITY.

Forth to the Trossachs, presently to be shut out by the Lennox Hills, until Glasgow is approached, when a foretaste of what is coming is afforded by a glimpse of the West Highlands to the right, a great rib of rock in the distance marking the southern boundary of Loch Lomond, the Queen of the Scottish Lakes. Glasgow, as a commercial centre, has in the rapidity and solidity of its expansion, hardly any parallel in the kingdom, and the interest which belongs to it archæologically and historically gives way to that of its industrial pursuits, which bring it in close touch with the markets of the world. The immediate approach to the city, dull enough in an artistic sense, is rendered interesting by the famous Cowlairs Incline, the train being lowered by wire

SCOTT MONUMENT, GLASGOW.

23

ropes along a steep tunnel nearly a mile long, which brings us to Queen Street Station.

George Square, on which the North British Station Hotel looks out, is a handsome open space, with a number of good statues and a Scott memorial, suggestive of the Nelson monument in Trafalgar Square, while it is surrounded by impressive architecture, notably the Municipal Buildings, which form its east side. All round one sees, in Glasgow, abundant evidences of wealth. To the practical character of the city the dark waters of the Clyde bear witness, as they rush through the heart of the streets, and it is difficult to credit the fact that less than twenty miles from this humming hive of trade lie the crystal waters of Loch Lomond, reflecting the beauties of the eternal hills.

BUCHANAN STREET, GLASGOW.

From Glasgow, a journey of about an hour by rail (still on the North British line), brings us to Craigendoran, the base of the new West Highland route, and the trip is well worth the taking on its own account, apart altogether from any ulterior intention in the way of touring. The moment the train emerges from the Queen Street tunnel, the Clyde comes into view, and it is closely followed all the way, changing its character from mile to mile. At first nothing but docks

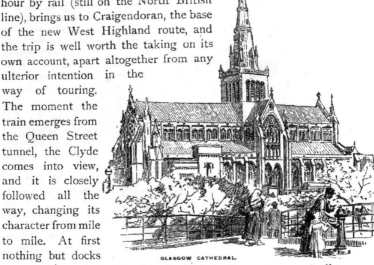

GLASGOW CATHEDRAL.

are seen, crowded with shipping; but the water gradually widens until it is a broad estuary of the sea. To the bustling docks succeed clanging ship-building yards, the riveters hammering on the plates of great vessels, standing in the stocks like the skeletons of mighty whales; but it is not until Partick is reached that the Clyde assumes the aspect

GEORGE SQUARE, GLASGOW.

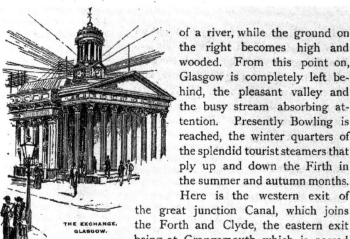

of a river, while the ground on the right becomes high and wooded. From this point on, Glasgow is completely left behind, the pleasant valley and the busy stream absorbing attention. Presently Bowling is reached, the winter quarters of the splendid tourist steamers that ply up and down the Firth in the summer and autumn months. Here is the western exit of the great junction Canal, which joins the Forth and Clyde, the eastern exit being at Grangemouth, which is passed on the way from Edinburgh to Glasgow. Pretty much the same route appears to have been followed by the Emperor Antoninus, when he built, in A.D. 140, the Roman Wall across the country, as a defence against the attacks of the Picts and Scots; for at Dunglass Point, a little further on, this barrier terminated in the Clyde, while traces of the same "Graham's Dyke" (*griem diog*—the strong trench) are also found near Falkirk. This wall, which was 36 miles long, is related to have been a rampart of earth 20 feet high and 24 feet thick, built on a stone foundation. At Dunglass may be seen the ruins of a castle formerly held by the Colquhouns of Luss, of whom we shall have more to tell; and on the Point stands an obelisk in memory of Henry Bell, the pioneer of steam navigation in Europe, of whom, also, there is more to say presently.

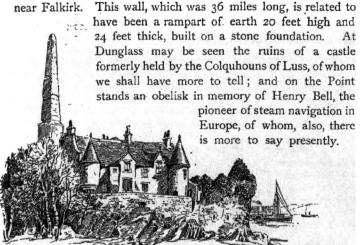

DUNGLASS CASTLE, AND BELL'S MONUMENT, BOWLING.

DUMBARTON CASTLE: NORTH SIDE.

A little beyond Dunglass comes the first strikingly picturesque point of the route—Dumbarton Castle, which stands out boldly on the left. Where the Leven, pouring from Loch Lomond, enters the Clyde, rises a great mass of basalt, a mile in circumference, and shaped like a kneeling dromedary, being formed in two "humps" rather than peaks. The higher of these "humps" is about 250 feet above the water level, while the lower is not much inferior. Around these summits, on the northern side, is built the Castle, with rambling battlements of considerable strength for the olden times, and to which access is gained by a narrow staircase, winding up steeply in the cleft between the two heights. From time immemorial the rock has been a stronghold, as was inevitable from its splendid defensive position—the remains of a Roman fort are seen on the top of the higher eminence, but the Castle itself is of more modern date. This Gibraltar of the Clyde cannot fail to rivet attention as it rears its vast bulk from the Firth like some leviathan dragging itself from

ARCHWAY ST. PATRICK'S, DUMBARTON.

the deep: records of it are left from every age. The Romans called it "Theodosia"; the Venerable Bede knew it as "Alcluid"; Macpherson's Ossian sang of it as "Balclutha," and blind Harry has handed down its praises.

From the time of the ancient Britons to the present day it has

C

carried a garrison, and in the days when Scotland had an independent navy, Dumbarton was one of the principal ports. In the time of William the Lion it was chief of the many strongholds of the Earl of Lennox; it was from the Castle that Mary Queen of Scots departed for the French court, and it is said that Sir William Wallace was imprisoned in one of the towers (now called after him), while the higher summit is known as "Wallace's Seat." Sir John Menteith was certainly the keeper, for Bruce took the Castle from under his control; and on the narrow gateway, that acts as portcullis to the ascent we have described, there remain

DUMBARTON CASTLE: SOUTH SIDE.

rudely carved on either side, heads of Wallace and Menteith—the latter with his finger in his cheek—the sign he gave when he betrayed the Scottish hero to the English. Many a siege and many an attack has it stood—the most interesting episode on record in its warlike history being its capture in 1571 by Captain Crawford, of Jordanhill, on behalf of the infant King, James the Sixth. With a handful of men this gallant soldier crept to the base of the impregnable rock with scaling ladders one misty and moonless night, selecting for the escalade the point where the rock was highest and least likely to be guarded. The first ladder broke under the ascending men, but the noise of their fall did not arouse the sentinels, owing to the remoteness of the attacking point. Captain Crawford then clambered up in person and succeeded in making the ladder fast to the roots of a tree growing on the face of the rock, and thus secured a footing for his little band. From a historical description of the affair we quote a graphic paragraph: "In scaling the second precipice another accident took place—one of the party, subject to epileptic fits, was seized by one of these attacks, brought on perhaps by terror, while he was in the act of climbing up the ladder. His illness made it impossible for him either to ascend or descend. To have slain the man would have been a cruel expedient, besides that, the fall of his body from the ladder might have alarmed the garrison. Crawford caused him, therefore, to be tied to the ladder, then all the rest descending, they turned the ladder, and thus mounted with ease over the body of the epileptic." Silently stabbing the careless sentinel when they reached the summit, the brave stormers surprised the sleeping garrison and obtained possession of the Castle by an almost bloodless victory.

STEAMERS AT BOWLING.

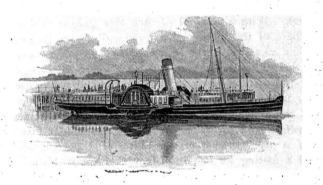

ALONG THE LOCHS.

AT Dalreoch, a little beyond Dumbarton, we have another reminder of the proximity of the picturesque, in a short branch line that strikes off on the right to Balloch, the most southerly point on Loch Lomond. A favourite excursion in the past, and one that will remain popular, is to run down by train to Balloch, take there one of the North British Steam Packet Company's steamers and circumnavigate the Loch, returning to Balloch after visiting Tarbet, Inversnaid and Ardlui, or, varying the route, to cross the narrow neck of land which intervenes between Tarbet and Arrochar, on the shores of Loch Long, sail down that Loch in one of the same Company's steamers to Craigendoran, re-joining the train there.

BALLOCH PIER.

Now that the railway is opened, there is a new day-trip, by rail to Ardlui, at the northern extremity of the Loch, and thence to Balloch by steamer, the charm of the excursion being thus doubled by its variety.

CRAIGENDORAN STATION.

A few minutes after leaving Dalreoch we pass Cardross, where stood the Castle in which King Robert the Bruce died, then Ardmore Point, a bold promontory on the left hand, extending into the Clyde, and immediately behind the line of beacons marking the termination of the jurisdiction of the Clyde Trustees, who are responsible for maintaining the navigation of 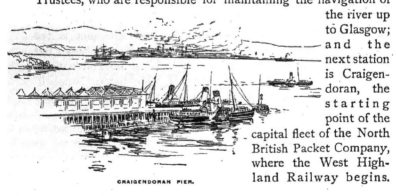 the river up to Glasgow; and the next station is Craigendoran, the starting point of the capital fleet of the North British Packet Company, where the West Highland Railway begins.

CRAIGENDORAN PIER.

The West Highland and the North British Railways overlap about a mile, the latter going on to Helensburgh. A few years ago it was intended to run the North British metals right down to Helensburgh pier,

BELL'S MONUMENT, HELENSBURGH.

in the middle of the parade, and there erect a station; but the town objected, on the ground that if passengers were carried straight through to the side of the steamers, the local shopkeepers would miss the orders that might be given had the passengers a little way to walk after leaving the train! This is an attitude worthy of ranking with that of Dumbarton, which rejected the proposal to make that town the port of Glasgow, by the construction of a harbour and docks, lest the consequent addition to the population should raise the price of butter and eggs. The North British Railway, however, built

GARELOCH.

a pier of its own at Craigendoran, and this pier is the terminus on the south of the West Highland Railway; but beyond the pier and the station there is, at present, nothing at Craigendoran. The landowner, Mr. Middleton Campbell, of Colgrain, prefers to retain his property intact and declines to let off ground for building purposes.

Helensburgh may therefore be regarded as the starting point of the West Highland Railway, for Craigendoran is merely a difference in name. The town (which was commenced in 1777 by Sir James Colquhoun of Luss, the great

32

GARELOCH-HEAD.

landowner of the district, and was named by him after his wife) is a pleasantly situated watering place, of about 9,000 inhabitants, lying at the mouth of the Gareloch and on the side of a gently sloping hill. It is the Brighton of Glasgow, the favourite resting-place of the busy City man, and is composed almost entirely of villas for summer occupation. There is no place on the Clyde where so many Glasgow men reside all the year; at present it partakes much more of this residential character than as a mere summer resort. Across the Firth of Clyde, about three and a half miles distant, lies grimy Greenock, "a crow facing a swan," as somebody has neatly put it. It is no wonder the weary Glaswegian finds it an agreeable relaxation to run down here whenever possible, to breathe the fresh sea air and contentedly watch the smoke of distant Greenock rising against the heights on the opposite shore, separated from its ceaseless energy by miles of sparkling water, lively with shipping. In past days Helensburgh was noted for its sea fishing, the remains still being shown of a wall, built out in the Firth, which was covered at high tide; and when the tide began to fall, men used to row out and open sluices so that the water was drained from the enclosure, leaving an extraordinary collection of fish, which was gathered into carts and sent off to market. But the proximity of Glasgow has now driven the fish away.

Peculiar interest attaches to Helensburgh from the fact

that it is the birthplace of steam navigation in Europe; Henry Bell, the father of the craft, having lived here for years and perfected his ideas, while it was from Glasgow to Greenock that his first steamer was run Bell was a Linlithgow man, born in 1767, and he began life as a stonemason, developed into a millwright, and finally became an engineer, serving under the famous Rennie in London, and afterwards working in a shipbuilding-yard at Borrowstounness. In 1790 he settled in Glasgow, and in 1807 came to Helensburgh, where his wife kept the "Baths" Hotel — still in existence as the "Queen's," the old name having become inappropriate. He had a strong mechanical bent, and devoted himself to experiments on the lines of applying steam-power to sailing vessels. As early as 1800 he suggested the principle to the British Government, but was treated as a visionary. In 1803 he again pressed the idea on the attention of the Government, but without avail. In exasperation he then communicated his theories, of how vessels might be propelled by steam, against both wind and tide, to all the Crowned Heads of Europe and to the President of the United States. Meanwhile, he himself was busy, and on the 12th January, 1812, the first British steamer was launched at Port Glasgow on the Clyde. It was built under his directions, and its engine was constructed according to his long thought out plan. This pioneer of European steamships was called the "Comet," on account of its extraordinary speed— which was five miles an hour! The vessel was 42 feet long and 11 feet broad, its draught was $5\frac{1}{2}$ feet, and its engine was of 3 horse-power, and there were two paddles on each side. The engine is preserved in the Kelvingrove Park, Glasgow. The curious may still see the "Comet," lying at Bowling (the station we passed before Dumbarton), but it is not precisely the vessel as launched, for a few years later, as other vessels were built with improvements, the length of the boat was increased to 60 feet, a new engine was put in, and a single paddle on each side took the place of the double, thus raising its sailing power to the appalling rate of six miles an hour! As a curiosity, we give an advertisement from a Glasgow newspaper of 5th August, 1812, the year of the launch :—

STEAM PASSAGE BOAT,

THE COMET,

BETWEEN GLASGOW, GREENOCK, AND HELENSBURGH,

FOR PASSENGERS ONLY.

THE Subscriber having, at much expense, fitted up a handsome Vessel to ply upon the RIVER CLYDE, between GLASGOW and GREENOCK—to sail by the power of Wind, Air and Steam— he intends that the Vessel shall leave the BROOMIELAW on TUESDAYS, THURSDAYS, and SATURDAYS, about Mid-day, or at such hour thereafter as may answer from the state of the Tide—and to leave GREENOCK on MONDAYS, WEDNESDAYS, and FRIDAYS, in the morning, to suit the Tide.

The elegance, comfort, safety, and speed of this Vessel requires only to be proved, to meet the approbation of the Public; and the Proprietor is determined to do everything in his power to merit public encouragement.

The terms are, for the present, fixed at 4s. for the best Cabin, and 3s. for the Second; but beyond these rates nothing is to be allowed to Servants, or any other person employed about the Vessel.

The Subscriber continues his Establishment at HELENSBURGH BATHS, the same as for years past, and a Vessel will be in readiness to convey PASSENGERS in the COMET from GREENOCK to HELENSBURGH.

Passengers by the COMET will receive information of the Hours of Sailing, by applying at Mr. HOUSTON'S OFFICE, Broomielaw; or Mr. THOMAS BLACKNEY'S, East Quay Head, Greenock.

HENRY BELL.

HELENSBURGH BATHS, *5th August*, 1812.

Visitors to the Queen's Hotel, which lies on the very shore of the Firth, may still see the remains of the pier at which the "Comet" lay when it arrived at the "Helensburgh Baths." To stand there and watch the great steamers go past by the hundred is a curious experience, for 1812 seems so close at hand that it is difficult to believe that this

HELENSBURGH, FROM CRAIGENDORAN PIER.

wonderful revolution in the world's progress has been achieved in fourscore years, and that the little pier at your feet was its starting point. Henry Bell died in his own hotel on 14th November, 1830, and was buried in the village of Row —the next station on the West Highland Railway. The obelisk to his memory at Dunglass Point we have already seen in passing; and there is another on Helensburgh esplanade, at the head of the pier, a graceful needle of polished red granite, one of the largest granite monoliths ever cut. It was erected in 1872, and the inscription testifies that Bell was "the first in Great Britain who was successful in practically applying steam power for the purpose of navigation." Fulton, in America, and others, had previously constructed experimental steamers, but it was Bell who made the steamship an actual commercial fact, and when he conceived the idea in 1786 he seems to have been first in the field.

From Helensburgh, or rather Craigendoran, there are good services of steamers to Dunoon, Rothesay, Gareloch-head, Arrochar, and other picturesque points, but our immediate concern is with the West Highland Railway, which we reach at Craigendoran.

UP THE LOCH, FROM GARELOCH-HEAD.

The railway passes round the north side of Helensburgh, looking down on the town, and affording a fine view of the Firth of Clyde at its widest part, across to Greenock and the "Tail of the Bank," an extensive sand shoal, and near to the

best anchorage in the Firth—the praises of which have been sung by a Greenock poet in the comprehensive lines :—

ARDENCAPEL CASTLE, HELENSBURGH.

Tail of the Bank! Arm of the Sea!
Where deep and shallow waters be!

a couplet that might be applied with equal felicity to almost any point in the neighbourhood; but Greenock has less poetry even than Glasgow. The country through which we are now passing is the estate of the Colquhoun family; the clan to which belongs the Luss district, on the western shore of Loch Lomond, having—not without many a conflict in the old clan days—gradually extended its lands far and wide. As may be seen by the contour of the Luss hills on the right, the line runs almost parallel with the famous Glen Fruin, sloping from the south-western extremity of Loch Lomond towards Gareloch-head, whither we are now making our way. This is the glen where the repeated slaughter of the Colquhouns, by their enemies the MacGregors, took place, as related in the preface to "Rob Roy." The Laird of Luss having slain two MacGregors for killing and eating one of his wedders, when they found themselves benighted in his country and denied hospitality, MacGregor marched from the banks of Loch Long with three or four hundred men, and met Sir Humphrey Colquhoun with his six or eight hundred men, in Glen Fruin, the "Glen of Sorrow." Thanks to the fact that the Colquhoun force was mainly cavalry, and that the boggy nature of the ground hampered its movements, the Clan MacGregor utterly routed their enemies, killing between two and three hundred, with a loss to themselves of only two men. In this fight, an ancestor of Rob Roy is said to have massacred, with his own dirk, a party of young divinity students from Glasgow, who had merely come out to see the fight, and a stone is still shown from which their blood can never be washed out. Sir Humphrey Colquhoun fled to the Castle of Banachar, near by, where he was soon after murdered in the vaults. This was in the reign of James the Sixth, and was the cause of the name of MacGregor being abolished by law, the widows of the slain, eleven score in number, appearing at Stirling in deep mourning, riding upon white palfreys, and each bearing her husband's bloody shirt on a spear, to invoke the King's vengeance. Readers of the "Lady of the Lake" will remember the stanza in the Boat Song, "Hail to the Chief":—

Proudly our pibroch has thrilled in Glen Fruin,
    And, Banachar's groans to our slogan replied :
Glen Luss and Ross-dhu, they are smoking in ruin,
    And the best of Loch Lomond lie dead on her side,
        Widow and Saxon maid
        Long shall lament our raid,
Think of Clan-Alpine with fear and with woe;
        Lennox and Leven-glen
        Shake when they hear agen,
"Roderigh Vich Alpine dhu, ho! ieroe!"

Hardly have we left Helensburgh when we find the train running close alongside the Gareloch, the line being cut on the hillside a considerable height above the water. The Gareloch is an arm of the Firth of Clyde, about six miles long and about a mile in width at the broadest part. On both sides it is shut in by low hills, right and left, covered with foliage; and so still and deep are its waters, and so free are the surrounding hills from magnetic influences, that it is the favourite place for the testing of ships' compasses, and is a popular anchorage for vessels lying up. About £3,000,000 worth of shipping, it is estimated, at present lies there rusting, including the hull of the steamship *Utopia*, which was sunk off Gibraltar by collision with one of Her Majesty's ships, and the raising of which was such a notable feat of engineering. Between Gareloch and Loch Long there is only a narrow promontory, hardly two miles across at most, and over the gentle range that shuts in the waters of the Gareloch rise the bold peaks of the crags that enclose the greater Loch. On the extremity of this promontory, opposite Helensburgh, may be seen Roseneath Castle, one of the seats of the Duke of Argyll, surrounded by a clump of trees, comprising "Adam and Eve," the two largest silver firs in Scotland, measuring twenty-three feet in girth five feet from the ground. All along the eastern side of the Loch are dotted beautiful villas in profusion, built on the hill slope

"THE COBBLER"
FROM NEAR GLEN DOUGLAS.

amid the woods, and clustered together at the points where stations have been fixed by the West Highland Railway — at Row (pronounced Rue, from the Gaelic derivation); at Shandon (where the well-known Hydropathic stands, overlooking one of the finest views in the valley); and at Gareloch-head, where the houses lie in a semi-circle around the head of the Loch. All along the course of the Loch it is a fairy retreat, silent, secluded, well sheltered and glowing with colour, the many tinted trees and the heather-clad slopes being reflected in the glassy water as in a mirror. So soft and beautiful is the landscape that it might have been the imagination of some gifted artist, combining to best advantage the graces of hill and wood and lake. But not a Royal Academician amongst them all can compete with Nature — a lesson that is impressed on one at every turning of this new road through a region

ARROCHAR, ON HEAD OF LOCH LONG,
FROM THE RAILWAY.

hitherto almost inaccess-
ible in many parts.

Leaving Gareloch-
head behind, the railway
ascends the ridge on which stands Whistlefield, one of the
healthiest and most romantic spots on the line. Here another
striking change of scene is met, the railway running to the
very verge of Loch Long, a magnificent piece of·water, narrow
but deep, which stretches from Strone some four-and-twenty
miles inland, curving round the promontory that shuts in the
Gareloch and forming the boundary between Argyllshire and
Dumbartonshire. If it be possible, Loch Long is even more
beautiful than the Gareloch, and it is infinitely more impressive.
From Whistlefield onwards, it is only about half a mile wide,
but instead of the low rounded heights that lie along the
Gareloch, the hills rise sheer from the water in stern outlines
far over-topping the previous eminences. Their summits and
shoulders are clad in purple heather and mosses of richest
brown and yellow, while along the water's edge lie belts of
trees, presenting a variety of greens of bewildering beauty.
Against the dark background of Scotch firs and oaks the
lighter tints of spruce and larch stand out with wonderful
vividness, while here and there gleams a clump of silver birches,
and in autumn the scarlet berries of the rowan throw in the touch
of red so dear to the heart of the artist. In the narrow waters
the hills seem to stretch down until the glowing slopes disappear

41

in the depths of the blue. The fascination of the scenery is that it never looks twice the same, changing into new aspects of beauty with every change of light and shade. A cloud passes over the sun, and the tones deepen and merge into new effects undreamt of a minute before; a slight shower descends, and the eye is bewitched with a new colouring. Where the railway meets the Loch is perhaps the most lovely in this respect, the point where Loch Goil branches off to the north-west leaving a steep promontory abutting on the Loch, with, at its foot,

LOOKING UP GLEN DOUGLAS. a small island which is a spot much favoured by the Loch fisherman. Whether this is the scene described in the ballad of "Lord Ullin's Daughter" is open to question, as that "dark and stormy water" lies a long way off, west of Mull, with "Ulva's Isle" adjoining, though, strictly speaking, the name is Loch-na-Keal and not Loch Goil; and our Loch Goil may well be the point intended by the poet, because three days from the mainland, opposite Mull, would bring "her father's men" to it.

After following for a short distance the shore of Loch Long, the railway bends to the right and plunges into the lonely Glen Mallin, the passenger sighing to think that the glories of the Loch have been abandoned. But the road has been diverted merely as a piece of good engineering, in order that a stretch of comparatively easy ground may be taken advantage of, and before many minutes have passed the line has curved back again to the water's edge. The country has now become wilder and more deserted, the railway being cut

BEN LOMOND, FROM ARROCHAR.

in the sides of steep hills, the embankments on the left dipping almost sheer into the water. On the further side of the Loch the hills become still grander and more precipitous. On their dark sides trees can hardly find root-hold, although the green bracken still flourishes to relieve the gloom of the black rocks and the brown heath. Their heads are reared to the clouds in a fine confusion of jagged peaks, that speaks a finely grim humour in the ironical observer who dubbed

TARBET HOTEL.

them "The Duke of Argyll's Bowling Green"—a name that still clings to the range. With the Bass Rock, or Ailsa Craig, for a ball, the ancient gods might have enjoyed a roaring game of skittles among those peaks. At the point where there is a passing place (the West Highland Railway being only a single line) Glen Douglas strikes off to the right, a rugged pass through the hills, which debouches on Loch Lomond opposite Rowardennan. A little further on to the

43

left, on the opposite side of Loch Long, may be seen the opening of a similar pass, Glen Croe, leading to Loch Fyne and Inverary.

Those who wish to visit that notable little town, the chief seat of the MacCallum More, will find at Tarbet a coach that will take them round the head of Loch Long, through Glen Croe, and round the head of Loch Fyne to Inverary. There they will be able to get on board the "Lord of the Isles,"

A BIT OF GENERAL WADE'S MILITARY ROAD, NEAR TARBET.

and sail back by Loch Fyne, Ardlamont, the Kyles of Bute, Rothesay, and Dunoon to Craigendoran. An alternative circular route from Inverary is to take coach from Strachur on Loch Fyne to the head of Loch Eck, sail down that Loch, the narrowest sheet of water in Scotland

ENTRANCE TO GLEN CROE, NEAR ARROCHAR.

in relation to its length of about seven miles, and coach to Dunoon, thence by steamer again to Craigendoran. At "Rest and be thankful," at the head of Glen Croe, the well-known doggerel rhyme is said to have been written:

> "Had you seen these roads before they were made
> You'd go down on your knees and bless General Wade"—

an enigmatical couplet smacking more of the sister island than of the usually clearly expressed Scottish diction.

BEN LOMOND, FROM LUSS.

About the point at which Glen Croe is seen branching off on the far side of Loch Long, a little further ahead on the same side of the water, the first of the real mountains comes in sight. This is Ben Arthur, or, as it is generally called, "The Cobbler," which rises to a height of 2,891 feet. Unless a hill reaches somewhere near 3,000 feet, it is a mere nonentity in these West Highlands, and although the peaks we have passed have been impressive, rising, as they do, almost perpendicularly from the waters that wash their bases, their height has ranged only from 1,500 to 2,000 feet. In the Midlands or Southern England, each one of them would be reckoned a marvel, but here it is difficult to ascertain even their names. "The Cobbler," however, commands respect at once, not only from its dominating height, but from its peculiar formation. Strictly speaking, there are two hills in one, Ben

Arthur, which has a rounded summit, and "The Cobbler," which terminates in two sharp peaks, split like a mitre. On the top of the southern peak is a great boulder, which, looked at from below on a clear day, has an unmistakable resemblance to a cobbler at work, bending over a shoe, with elbows extended as he stitches the leather. On the northern peak is a companion boulder, which has a certain likeness to an old woman, and which is known as Jean, his wife. There is a sort of fairy tale about the pair: and a thin white stream that trickles down the side of the hill is supposed to be a bowl of milk that she has spilt. Beyond rise the heads of four other mountains which form, with "The Cobbler," what are known as the Arrochar Alps—

A BIT OF THE ROAD THROUGH THE TROSSACHS.

Ben Crois (2,785 feet), Ben Ime (3,318 feet), Ben Vane (3,002 feet), and Ben Voirlich (3,092 feet). We are now at the head of the Loch, and the hills gather in closely all around, with brown summits and purple flanks, glowing warmly in the sun, or looming darkly in the shadow, hardly a tree to be seen, except around the Loch itself. As the line curves to the right, away from the water, the mighty bulk of Ben Lomond is descried on that side, close by, as the train pulls up at Arrochar and Tarbet Station, about twenty miles from Craigendoran.

This is the most individual point on the whole route, for the station lies midway between Loch Long, the great salt water·estuary, and Loch Lomond, the vast fresh water lake, only about three-quarters of a mile apart, for the two great sheets of water converge and almost meet, the former slanting to the north-east and the latter to the north-west. A better spot for the tourist to break his journey could not be imagined, for he is in the very heart of the picturesque; and

BEN LOMOND, FROM ARROCHAR STATION.

has, moreover, every facility for accommodation. In Arrochar, which is a pleasant little village, lying at the head of Loch Long, and facing "The Cobbler," there is a comfortable inn; and at Tarbet, a cluster of houses on the shore of Loch Lomond, there is a hotel that is positively palatial, with bedrooms for nearly a hundred guests. It is a surprise to find such a luxurious resting place in the wilds, but the explanation is that Tarbet is the popular stopping point with the steamers that ply on Loch Lomond, and in summer the holiday guest taxes the accommodation to the full. How

47

THE MANSE BURN, ARROCHAR.

the tourist whose time is limited may make a round trip *via* Inverary we have just shown, and a still shorter method will be to take steamer at Arrochar and sail back to Dunoon, traversing by water the route he has covered by land, with the new attraction thrown in of that part of Loch Long hidden from the railway by the peninsula which separates it from the Gareloch—a very enjoyable one-day trip.

Loch Long being an arm of the Firth of Clyde, its level is that of the sea, but Loch Lomond lies twenty-two feet higher. In shape it may be compared to a Malay *crease* or dagger, the waving blade being about fourteen miles long and of a breadth ranging from half a mile to a mile and a half; while the hilt, about eight miles long, is some five miles wide at the broadest part. Its depth is as variable as its width, being measured by hundreds of feet at the northern end, where the vast flood is pent by granite mountains, and by tens of feet only at the southern extremity, where it is spread over a less precipitous country; the maximum depth is at Craigenarden, being 660 feet. The superficial area of the lake is about twenty thousand acres, and it is by far the largest fresh-water loch in Scotland. As Christopher North exclaims, "Loch Lomond is a sea! Along its shores you might voyage in your swift schooner, with shifting breezes, all a summer's day, nor at sunset, when you dropped anchor, have seen half the beautiful wonders." Wordsworth, who visited the locality with Coleridge in 1803, thought "the proportion of diffused water was too great," a sentiment that brought old Christopher down on him in a fine torrent of indignation. "It is out of our power," he

LOCH LOMOND, FROM ABOVE LUSS.

says, "to look on Loch Lomond without a feeling of perfection. The 'diffusion of water' is indeed great; but in what a world it floats! At first sight of it, how our soul expands! The sudden revelation of such majestic beauty, wide as it is, and extending afar, inspires us with a power of comprehending it all."

Totally distinct in character are the two sections of the Loch, the narrow and the wide. From the northern end down to Luss, the water is hemmed in on both sides by mighty hills, springing from the water and mounting to the sky so steeply that it looks as if a boulder started from the summit of any one of them would never cease its downward rush until it plunged into the Loch. "The lake is felt to belong to them— to be subjected to their will—and that is capricious; for some-

TARBET PIER.

times they suddenly blacken it when at its brightest, and sometimes when its gloom is like that of the grave, as if at their bidding, all is light." From Luss southwards the scene is softer, the greys and browns of rock and lichen giving place to a rich green, the eminences that bound the Loch becoming gentle and rounded until the landscape is suggestive of the English Lakes, "the magnificent expanse broken with un-numbered isles, and the shores diversified with jutting cape and far-shooting peninsula, enclosing sweet separate seclusions, each in itself a loch."

At Tarbet you are well placed for studying the beauties of Loch Lomond. On the further shore Ben Lomond heaves up its gigantic form, shoulder on shoulder, crowned by a grand pyramidal summit of bare rock, the whole mountain without anything to break the bold outlines of the enormous mass, brilliant in purples

COLQUHOUN.   MAC FARLANE.   MAC GREGOR.

and browns and darkest greens. Ben Lomond, with its altitude of 3,192 feet, is not quite so lofty as Ben Ime, beyond Arrochar, but its noble formation, and its place on the very verge of the Loch, impart to it a peculiar grandeur, and towering above the lesser hills by its side, its head lost in the clouds, it stands a veritable King. One of the finest views of the Loch is to be obtained by driving down from Tarbet, on a road that winds level with the water at the foot of the hills, to where Glen Douglas spreads open from Loch Long. Southward the Thirty Islands may be seen opening out in all their beauty of foliage, over the widening Loch; while northwards the water narrows, its shores growing in sternness as far as the eye can penetrate, while over all rise the two great mountains, Ben Lomond and Ben Voirlich. For those who wish to thoroughly explore this magnificent Loch, Tarbet is the natural starting point, for the pier is a regular calling place for the steamers that ply on the Loch, from north to south and from east to west. For those who prefer to drive, there is an excellent road by the Loch-side all the way from Balloch at the

BRIDGE DIVIDING ARGYLLSHIRE AND DUMBARTONSHIRE, HEAD OF LOCH LONG.

south end of the Lake to Ardlui at the northern end, along the western shore. But from Tarbet to Ardlui the railway is better than the road, the two running almost parallel, while the railway commands a finer view by being a little higher up the hillside.

All around Arrochar and Tarbet, and a long way north along the Loch, was the country of the Clan MacFarlane, a wild race of freebooters whose habit of descending on the Lowlands by night gave the local name of "MacFarlane's lantern" to the moon. On the eastern side of the Loch lies the MacGregors' country—the home of the Gregarach or Clan Alpine, from which they were so ruthlessly driven out when their very name was proscribed and their possessions confiscated on account of their turbulence. When the Queen, some twenty years ago, wished to make a collection of paintings of representative clansmen in full tartan,

THE ONLY TUNNEL.

it was from Luss that a Colquhoun was taken as model, from Arrochar a MacFarlane, and from Inversnaid, on the opposite side of the Loch a few miles beyond Tarbet, a MacGregor—a fact that brings home to us how deeply plunged into the

51

Highlands we are at Tarbet. Still more is this impressed upon us when, looking across the water, to the mountains of Stirlingshire, we are reminded at various points that the wild hills opposite are Rob Roy's country. About a mile below Tarbet, but on the further side of the Loch, may be seen rising from the water, "Rob Roy's Prison," an arch-shaped cavern formed by masses of fallen rock. Here it was the pleasant custom of the outlaw to interview his captives. If they proved refractory they were lowered into the Loch by a rope and further interrogated after each dip until they proved more complaisant. Little wonder that Andrew Fairservice said, "To gang into Rob Roy's country is a mere tempting o' Providence." Scott, in his famous novel, has located his scenes for the most part further east, around and beyond Aberfoyle, but the eastern shore of Loch Lomond was the most

A WEST HIGHLAND STATION (ARROCHAR AND TARBET).

frequent and principal stronghold of the notorious freebooter. When this is remembered, the rugged land on which we look assumes a new aspect, for it requires no great effort of the imagination to picture Rob Roy and his followers stealing along the hillsides to some foray. Just as the country looked then, it looks now, for there is not a sign of habitation about those dark slopes and beetling crags. There is nothing to jar with the fancy, for it was the close proximity of civilisation in his day that brought into such strong relief his lawless character. As Scott puts it, "He owed his fame in a great measure to his residing on the very verge of the Highlands, and playing such pranks in the beginning of the 18th century as are usually ascribed to Robin Hood in the middle ages,— and that within forty miles of Glasgow, a great commercial city, the seat of a learned university. Thus a character like his, blending the wild virtues, the subtle policy, and unrestrained license of an American Indian, was flourishing in Scotland during the Augustan age of Queen Anne and

George I." Several lineal descendants of Rob Roy are yet to be found in the neighbourhood, and are regarded with a certain respect to this day. Even Wordsworth asserts with enthusiasm that he was no mere commonplace reiver, singing at his grave:—

"For thou, although with some wild thoughts,
Wild Chieftain of a savage Clan!
Hadst this to boast of—thou didst love
The LIBERTY of man.

"And had it been thy lot to live
With us who now behold the light,
Thou wouldst have nobly stirred thyself,
And battled for the Right."

CALLING THE FERRY, LOCH LOMOND.

Leaving Tarbet, the railway follows the windings of the Loch, running along a hill-side well wooded at the base with oak and fir, spruce and larch, birch and the mountain ash, and with an undergrowth of almost tropical luxuriance— so warm and moist is the atmosphere in the heat of summer. This is the Kenmore Wood, which extends along the Loch from about the point where Tarbet Island is passed to Inveruglas, some three miles up. Before reaching that point, Inversnaid is seen on the opposite side of the Loch—where travellers strike off for the land of the "Lady of the Lake," being carried across by steamer from Tarbet. Apart from these periodical steamers, the communication is by ferry, which is the regular mode of transit for the natives and the resident doctor of the district, who has to cover an immense stretch of country. To see the method of calling the ferry-boat from the hotel on the other side brings forcibly to one's mind the primitive methods of the district. At Tarbet there is an old coach-horn, which is borrowed by the favoured few as they pass through the village, if they are presently

LOCH LOMOND, FROM THE RAILWAY AT ARDLUI.

returning, and from its brazen lungs wild blasts are sent across the water until the boat is seen to be coming. But the general device is to light a fire on the bank and pile on heather and twigs until a column of smoke is raised that can be seen across the mile and a quarter of water intervening. In dry weather this is not a matter of much difficulty, but in wet weather it is a hard task. To complete the picture of the lonely character of the country, we may mention that on the hill-side, a little lower than Inversnaid, is a shieling where lives an old tailor, far from any human habitation, and on him the neighbour-hood for miles around depends. The crofters, gamekeepers, and shepherds send the wool of their own sheep to Galashiels or Hawick, and when it returns in the form of tweed, they send for this sartorial hermit. He comes with his goose and his board, and puts up in the house of his customer until the required clothes are completed, returning then to his lonely

hut overlooking the Loch. Even the flat-bottomed ferry-boat has to watch an opportunity for crossing the Loch, as these inland waters are very treacherous, being subject to sudden squalls from the hills. At one moment the water is sparkling calmly in the sun ; the next the spin-drift is careering over the surface, sucked up by a whirlwind. Yet it is on record that one Sunday, during the construction of the line, a thirsty Irish navvy, a little further up the Loch, lashed two planks together and paddled across for two miles to Inversnaid in order to get a glass of beer !

UPPER AND LOWER FALLS, INVERSNAID.

INVERSNAID HOTEL AND PIER.

For a moment let us leave the course of the railway, and glance at the route of the traveller who abandons the West Highland Line at Tarbet in order to visit the Trossachs. From Tarbet a steamer carries him across to Inversnaid, and as that place is approached a fine view is obtained of the Arklet Falls, tumbling into the waters of the Loch. The stream pours from Loch Arklet, and has been appropriated as part of the water supply of Glasgow, and at Inversnaid descends sharply in a beautiful cascade of two steps—a short rush over the face of the black rock, a brief pause, and then a deep plunge to Loch Lomond. The foaming water breaks through a narrow and beautiful ravine, embowered in foliage, and the sudden silvery flash of the cascade on the brown slopes of

LOCH KATRINE, FROM STRONACHLACHER PIER.

the Loch-side is very striking, although the fall is of no great magnitude. This is the scene celebrated in Wordsworth's "Highland Girl."

"Sweet Highland Girl! a very shower
Of beauty is thy earthly dower!
And these grey rocks; that household lawn;
These trees, a veil just half withdrawn;
This fall of water that doth make
A murmur near the silent lake;
This little bay; a quiet road
That holds in shelter thy abode—
In truth, together do you seem
Like something fashioned in a dream;
.   .   .   .   . the cabin small,
The lake, the bay, the waterfall;
And Thee, the Spirit of them all."

ON LOCH EARN.

Where the "cabin small" stood, there is now a good hotel, furnishing Dr. Johnson's item in his estimate of a beautiful view, and affording excellent refreshment for the inner man before the five-mile journey to Loch Katrine is entered upon.

After the beauties of the neighbourhood have been explored, the tourist may take a coach, which makes its way up Glen Arklet by a winding road, curving up the hillside.

Looking backwards, as the summit is reached, a magnificent view is obtained of the Arrochar Alps, their shapely conical summits towering into the blue. Furthest south is Ben Crois, then come Ben Ime, Ben Vane and Ben Voirlich (which, by the way, must not be confounded with the Perthshire Ben of the same name overlooking Loch Earn). A little further,

at the mouth of the glen that runs at right angles to Glen Arklet, is the site (marked by a farmhouse) of the old fort established here in 1713 to keep Rob Roy and his clan in check, commanding the routes from the south likely to be used in the return from forays. The tombstones of the soldiers who died in the garrison may still be seen near by. The fort stood upon Rob Roy's original property of

BRIGDE OF FORTH, ABERFOYLE.

Inversnaid, and was at one time commanded by Captain Wolfe, who, as General Wolfe, became the conqueror of Quebec. Scott thus summarises the history of the fort:—"Even this military establishment could not bridle the restless MacGregor. He contrived to surprise the little fort, disarm the soldiers, and destroy the fortifications. It was afterwards re-established, and again taken by the MacGregors under Rob Roy's nephew, Ghlune Dhu, previous to the insurrection of 1745-6. Finally, the fort of Inversnaid was a third time repaired, after the extinction of civil discord. It is now (1817) totally dismantled." He adds: "About 1792, when the author chanced to pass that way, a garrison, consisting of a single veteran, was still maintained at Inversnaid. The venerable warder was reaping his barley croft in all peace and tranquillity, and when we asked admittance to repose ourselves, he told us we would find the key of *the Fort* under the door." Yet it was only some fifty years before, that Rob Roy died: so great is the change that can be wrought in half a century.

About three miles from Inversnaid, Loch Arklet is reached, a dark sheet of water, a mile long by half a mile wide, lying in the shadow of Ben Lomond, and its scenery having much of the gentle beauty of the neighbouring loch. It is famous for its trout. It was at the south-western end of this Loch, in a house still pointed out, that Helen MacGregor, the wife of Rob Roy, was born, that "woman of fierce and haughty temper," who did so much to nurse the violent tendencies of her husband. Near by is another hut—an early residence of Rob Roy himself. Soon after leaving Loch Arklet, a road branches off on the right to Aberfoyle, by the way of Loch Chon and Loch Ard, while on the left may be seen, in the distance, the heights that mark Glen Gyle, the ancient seat of the chiefs of the Clan MacGregor, lying at the north-western extremity of Loch Katrine. Then burst upon the sight the beauties of that Loch, looked down upon by three great hills— to the right, Ben Venue (2,393 feet); in front, Ben A'an (1,500 feet); and to the left front, Ben Ledi (2,875). Descending rapidly to Loch Katrine, the coach draws up at Stronachlacher Hotel, a house built on the shore in the style

of a Swiss châlet. The western portion of Loch Katrine is comparatively uninteresting; but, nevertheless, the view from Stronachlacher is magnificent, as the eye follows the course of the gleaming water, in which the surrounding hills seem to stand inverted, into the very heart of the Perthshire Highlands. All around is the "Lady of the Lake" country, every hill, every glen, every island, every turning of the loch being familiar by name, to readers of Scott. Tempting though

BEN A'AN AND ELLEN'S ISLE.

ELLEN'S ISLE AND BEN VENUE.

the task would be, we cannot further pursue this divergence from the West Highland Railway; but must leave the tourist to make his own way by steamer along Loch Katrine, thence through the glorious Trossachs, and on by Loch Achray and

LOCH ARKLET.

Loch Vennachar to Callander, where he will find a railway again; or by coach to the "Clachan of Aberfoyle," where is the station of a branch of the North British Railway, which will take him back to Edinburgh or Glasgow.

We return now to the West Highland Railway, which we quitted in the spirit when the white falls of Arklet caught our vision across the broad waters of Loch Lomond, like a finger-post pointing to Loch Katrine. A short distance on, and the line crosses, by a high viaduct, the Inveruglas, a mountain torrent that pours down from Loch Sloy, a narrow sheet of water shut in by

GLIMPSE OF BEN VENUE AND LOCH ARKLET.

the rocky sides of Ben Voirlich on the one hand and Ben Dhu on the other. For those who have time to spare, it is well worth the walk of three miles up the glen to see this gloomy mountain lake, from which the MacFarlanes took their slogan, or war-cry. Here the clan gathered for war, and the name signifies " the lake of the host." Where the Inveruglas Water enters Loch Lomond is a pretty little wooded island, known as Wallace's Isle, there being a vague tra-

ARROCHAR ALPS, FROM LOCH KATRINE.

dition that the Scottish hero once hid there when pursued. A little further up lies another island on the Loch, the ruins of an old Highland keep showing through the trees. This is Inveruglas Isle, and the castle was a stronghold of the Mac-Farlanes. In the old clan days, when warfare was conducted by means of the claymore and the bow and arrow, or at best by the flint-lock gun, such a fastness as this was virtually impregnable. Not only could it not be taken by assault, but it could not be starved out. There was water in plenty at hand, and provisions could be brought at night by boat, for it would have been impossible to guard the whole of Loch Lomond-side.

About a mile beyond Inversnaid, on the same side of the

LOCH ARD, ABERFOYLE.

Loch, is Rob Roy's Cave. Here the Loch narrows, and a good view of the Cave may be obtained from Craigenarden Viaduct. As the hills on both shores draw closer, their sides become steeper and more rugged, rising in stern precipices from the water. On the face of one of these dark and forbidding crags, near the water's edge, the Cave is sunk in the rock a man's height, access being obtained by means of a ladder. It is a romantic, but not an alluring residence; and many a time did Rob Roy lie concealed there when his enemies were hot on his track. It is said that Robert the Bruce also hid here, after the battle of Dalry in 1306. The

wild district in which the Cave is situated is Craig Royston, of which Rob Roy was himself the laird, and it lies on the verge of the lands of the Duke of Montrose, the nobleman who was at first the patron of Rob Roy, and afterwards his most bitter foe.

THE BACK OF BEN LOMOND.

Readers will remember the stirring verse in Scott's "MacGregor's Gathering," where the clan vows eternal revenge on those who had caused them to be dispossessed of their estates:—

> "Through the depths of Loch Katrine the steed shall career,
> O'er the peak of Ben Lomond the galley shall steer,
> And the rocks of Craig Royston like icicles melt,
> Ere our wrongs be forgot, or our vengeance unfelt!"

None of the three events has taken place; and the MacGregors are now as peaceable as the rest of us.

A mile and a half further up the Loch, opposite the proud crest of Ben Voirlich, where the wooded hills drawing still closer, narrows the Loch to a quarter of a mile, lies a third island, the Isle of Vou, on which is another ruin. The name means "the island of stores," and as it lies midway between the lands of the MacFarlanes and the MacGregors, it was probably a place where the two clans interchanged their spoils by barter. Some, on the other hand, are inclined

to think that the old black ruin, lying amongst the verdant larch and spruce, was a priory, and in support of this theory they bring forward a curious argument. On the little island there grows, in luxuriant profusion, the daffodil, a flower found nowhere else in the neighbourhood; and it is pointed out that wherever the daffodil flourishes in these Highland solitudes, it always is found that in some former time there has been settled some religious establishment—the flower having been cultivated for especial use for Easter and other festivals of the Church.

An interesting object, in more modern Church history, is to be seen after turning the point below which the Island of Vou lies. This is the famous Pulpit Rock, which stands in a hollow on the right, on the margin of the Loch. It is an enormous isolated boulder, "standing four-square to all the winds that blow," 45 feet in height, 70 in width, and 70 in breadth, a mass of rock estimated to weigh twenty thousand tons. The nearest minister is at Arrochar, some ten or twelve miles distant by road, and the inhabitants of the district at the foot of Ben Voirlich and the head of the Loch, complained that they had no sufficient spiritual instruction. "Build me a pulpit and vestry," said the minister of Arrochar, "and I will come at certain dates and preach to you." Thereupon the people took hammer and chisel in hand,

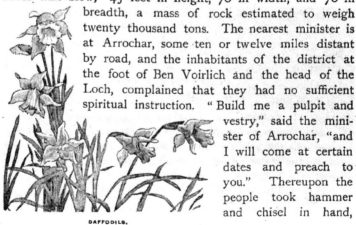

DAFFODILS.

64

and quarried out of the face of this huge rock a square chamber, reached by a flight of steps. To the opening a door was hinged, and the vestry was complete. When the door was opened the pulpit also was complete, the preacher standing on the threshold of this cell in the heart of the great rock, while the people sat below, on seats of cut sod, and listened to the Word, Ben Voirlich towering behind the pulpit and the quiet Loch gleaming behind the worshippers. The scene must have been wonderfully impressive, and typical of earnest Scottish religion. To erect a less permanent pulpit would have been a less laborious task; but those old Highlanders felt they were making a temple of God, and that nothing could be so fitting as to carve out from the solid rock a place

A HIGHLAND GLEN.

from which the Gospel might be taught. Looking on that great rock, rearing its altar amid the silent grandeur of mountain and loch, one feels carried back far into the times of the Old Testament.

Opposite the Pulpit Rock, on the eastern side of the Loch, near the Doune Farm, there is a point where three counties meet —Dumbartonshire (in which we have hitherto been travelling almost since leaving Glasgow), which curves round the head of the Loch; Stirlingshire, which has faced us on the right since we reached Tarbet; and Perthshire, which lies north and east, and which we are soon to enter. There is a stone at this point on which three men from different counties can sit, hand-in-hand, each in his own shire. About a mile and a half beyond the Pulpit Rock, the train draws up at Ardlui, twenty-seven miles from Craigendoran, and eight miles from Arrochar and Tarbet. Those who are making only a day trip will find a steamer here to take them the whole length of Loch Lomond, down to Balloch, whence Glasgow can readily be reached by railway.

HEAD OF LOCH LOMOND, NEAR ARDLUI

AMONG THE HILLS

GLEN FALLOCH.

A RDLUI is the most minute of villages, lying at the
head of Loch Lomond; but it possesses a good hotel,
thanks to the fact that it is a calling point for the steamers'
on the Loch. It is situated at the entrance to Glen Falloch—
"the hidden glen," so called from the sudden bend the valley
takes a little further up, conveying the impression that it is
a *cul-de-sac*, whereas it has hardly begun. Down the glen
runs the River Falloch, while on each side rise what Scott
has described as "dusky mountains," into the midst of which
the railway, following the picturesque stream, proceeds along
the glen. The last of the great inland lochs is left behind,
but there are plenty of smaller lakes yet to be passed ere we
reach Fort William. For a space, however, the scene is quite
changed; we have plunged into a maze of mountains, the
threading of which forms the second stage of the journey.

Glen Falloch is a narrow but well-wooded valley, the green of the glen and the brown of the hills forming a beautiful contrast, while the gleam of the river completes the picture. We may recall " The Fate of Mac-Gregor," by James Hogg, the Ettrick Shepherd, in which reference is made to the glen :—

"MacGregor, MacGregor, remember our foemen ;
The moon rises broad from the brow of Ben Lomond ;
The Clans are impatient, and chide thy delay ;
Arise, let us bound to Glen Lyon away !
"Stern scowled the MacGregor ; then silent and sullen,
He turned his red eye to the braes of Strathfillan ;
'Go, Malcolm, to sleep; let the Clans be dismissed;
The Campbells this night for MacGregor must rest.'"

PART OF OLD CALEDONIAN FOREST, GLEN FALLOCH.

The Chief goes on to tell Malcolm that in the night he had been visited by a wraith, the spirit of a fair dame, of whose fate a terrible tale could be related, and that he had vowed a great oath :—

"Ere the shadow fell east from the pile,
To meet her alone by the brook of Glen Gyle.
She told me, and turned my chilled heart to a stone,
The glory and name of MacGregor were gone:
That the pine, which for ages had shed a bright halo
Afar on the mountains of Highland Glen Falo,
Should wither and fall ere the turn of yon moon,
Smit through by the canker of hated Colquhoun :
That a feast on MacGregors each day should be common
For years to the eagles of Lennox and Lomond."

Glen Falo is the poet's corruption of Glen Falloch ; Glen Gyle is the glen we have already described, sloping from the north-western extremity of Loch Katrine almost to Ardlui; Strathfillan is a few miles further along the line at Crianlarich; and Glen Lyon we see a few miles beyond that.

We are now in a region of picturesque waterfalls, the first of which is the Garabal Fall, on the left, about a mile above Ardlui. A mountain torrent, coming down the Strath Dubhuisge, or "valley of the black water," from a tarn at the foot of Ben Damhain, breaks over the shoulder of Garabal Hill, and pours foaming down an almost perpendicular slope of about sixty feet. Unfortunately the Fall is not visible from the railway; but those who break their journey at Ardlui should not miss it. Passengers, however, can well afford to lose this one spectacle, for when Inverarnan is reached, about two miles from Ardlui, a couple of still finer cascades are to be seen, one on either hand. On the left the Arnan Water comes boiling down in the dip between two hills, and hurls itself over a steep slope about a hundred feet in depth, swerving to the left, and swinging round an obstructing eminence to join the River Falloch. On the right the waterfall is still more beautiful—the Falls of Ben-y-Glass. Down a narrow corrie, fringed with birch and oak, from the crest of a hill rising steeply from the glen, a mountain torrent descends, invisible until it suddenly breaks out on the face of a cliff, in a fine cascade, like a huge vein of white quartz. It falls in three branches, two clinging round either side of a great projecting boulder, spreading over the black rock like delicate lace, while to the left a wide jet of foam flashes out, rushing down the "Devil's Staircase" to join the other branches, the whole stream falling in a silver sheet to a basin about 120 feet below, at the foot of the precipice. When the Lammas floods are on, in August, the force of the fall is so great that the spray is sent seething up to a considerable height, drifting in a curtain of mist before the cascade ; but so sheer is the fall of the water down the dark crag that it does not seem to move at all.

Inverarnan, which lies on the bank of the Falloch, consists of only a few houses, the principal being the old hotel, which, during the construction of the line, was turned into a residence for the engineers engaged. The steamers on Loch Lomond used to come up to Inverarnan, before the pier at Ardlui was built, and the hotel was the old posting establishment Beside it can be seen the little artificial basin where the vessels lay. From Inverarnan coaches used to run all the way to Fort William, Oban, and

FALLS OF FALLOCH.

Ballachulish—cruel journeys in winter time on an outside seat, perched on the top of your luggage!

A short distance above Inverarnan the boundary of Dumbartonshire is crossed, and the line enters Perthshire, the glen becoming more rugged as Loch Lomond is left behind. Stirlingshire was lost sight of, on the east side of the Loch, when we passed the Island of Vou. Since then it has been Dumbartonshire, both on right and left, and now it is Perthshire, on both hands, until about a mile beyond Tyndrum. Soon after entering Perthshire, at the point where the glen takes a sharp bend to the right, the railway crosses a considerable mountain torrent, the Dubh Eas, the main tributary of the Falloch, on a viaduct which is the highest on the line, although not the longest. There are two noteworthy features about this Glen Falloch viaduct: firstly, that the piers on which it stands, like those of several lower viaducts on the line, are built of concrete, a novelty in railway engineering, although that material is largely used for other engineering purposes; and secondly, that the height, from the water, of the rails on the centre span, namely 143 feet,

LOCH EARN HEAD.

is only a few feet less than the similar dimension of the Forth Bridge.

The line continues to follow the River Falloch up the glen between steep mountain slopes, rich in heather and broom, but bare of trees. Soon after leaving Inverarnan, an interesting object presents itself—a boulder of peculiar formation, standing on a gentle eminence on the west side of the stream. This is the Clach-na-Breton, or, as it is generally called, the "Mortar Stone," its shape being exactly like that piece of artillery standing in position. It was here that Robert the Bruce paused to reconnoitre, in his flight after

GLEN OGLE, TOWARDS LOCH EARN HEAD.

71

FINLARIG CASTLE, LOCH TAY.

his defeat by the M'Dougals of Lorn, in Strathfillan, otherwise known as the Battle of Dalry—or, to write more correctly, Dail Righ, "the King's Field." The scene of the fight is near Tyndrum, a station a few miles further north. When he reached the "Mortar Stone," and stopped to see whether immediate pursuit had been shaken off, Bruce was on his way to the fastnesses of Loch Lomond; and, as already recorded, he found shelter in "Rob Roy's Cave" at Craig Royston—some four centuries before the bold outlaw was born. In the neighbourhood of this "Mortar Stone" there used to be an old Highland clachan, from which the stone took its Gaelic name; and in cutting the line the engineers found here the remains of furnaces for smelting iron —northwards, on Rannoch Moor, similar furnaces were also found.

IN GLEN OGLE.

In passing, a good view is obtained of the Falls of

72

Falloch, the upper Falls in particular being notably picturesque. The stream is so close-confined above the Falls, into a linn about ten feet wide, deep sunk in the solid rock, that in times of spate the water has been known to rise fifteen feet. The force of the pent current may, therefore, be imagined, and it hurls over the rock, where the bed of the stream dips, in a smother of foam, familiarly known as "Rob Roy's Bath." At the side of the main torrent, a smaller branch of the Falls has carved a round basin in the rock, by the constant churning of stones from the river bed, and this is called "Rob Roy's Soap Dish." Looking back at this point, a magnificent view of the mountains that close around the head of Loch Lomond is obtained, with Ben Voirlich towering over all. The stream, which was widely spread at the opening of the valley, is now confined within narrow banks; the glen has contracted into a mere mountain pass, and the scenery becomes wilder every mile. Hitherto the trees fringing the watercourse have been mostly larch, birch, spruce and rowan, soft in tone and feathery in foliage, with here and there an oak. But we are now approaching Crianlarich, the point where even the oak gives way to the Scotch fir, which finds congenial soil in the stern country coming.

To that noble national tree we are given an impressive introduction about five miles from Inverarnan —for, scattered along the hillside, on the east bank of the Falloch, lies a remnant of the ancient Caledonian Forest. Such trees are worth travelling many a mile to see, for they are superb specimens of the race that can cling to rocky hillsides where nothing else could find roothold, and flourish through century on century of

REMNANT OF THE CALEDONIAN FOREST.

RIVER DOCHART, KILLIN.

storm. These aged veterans are not the tall and symmetrical pines that we find in sheltered forests, soaring from
the ground, straight and high as a mast; for their great
trunks and branches are gnarled and twisted as if by some
fierce agony, each tree a Laocoon of the forest, while storms

KILLIN. BEN LAWERS IN DISTANCE.

that may have
raved down the
glen hundreds of
years ago, have
half uprooted
many of them,
leaving them
leaning down
the hillside in
curious con-
tortions, their
roots partly
dragged from

MILL ON THE DOCHART.

the ground, but more firmly fixed than ever at the un-
natural angle. Each tree seems to have been watered
with the Elixir of Life, and stands there weird as the
Wandering Jew, defying time and tempest to dull the warm
red glow of trunk and branch, or the dark but vivid green
of its clustered spines. It is curious to reflect that in past
ages the whole of the country side was covered with a vast
forest, of which these are the sparse remnants, where the
wolf howled and the wild boar grunted. "What happened
of old," asks Christopher North, "to the aboriginal Forests
of Scotland, that they have almost perished, leaving to bear
witness what
they were, such
survivors?
They were
chiefly des-
troyed by fire.
What power
could extin-
guish chance-
kindled con-
flagrations,
when sailing
before the
wind? And,
no doubt, fire

LOCH TAY PIER.

LOCH AWE.

was set to clear the country at once of wolves, wild-boars, outlaws, and Scotch firs. Tradition yet tells of such burnings; and, if we mistake not, the pines found in the Scottish mosses, the logs and the stocks, all show that they were destroyed by Vulcan, though Neptune buried them in the quagmires. Storms, no doubt, often levelled them by thousands; but had millions so fallen they had never been missed; and one Element only—which has been often fearfully commissioned—could achieve the work."

As we pass these scattered relics of the dead past, we see rising on the right a triangular hill, called Cruach Ardran, which possesses the peculiar distinction that each of its three faces supplies a separate great river. On the west it helps to swell the Falloch, which runs into Loch Lomond, obtaining

IN GLEN DOCHART.

exit by the Leven and joining the Clyde at its mouth; on the east it drains into the Lochlarig, thence by Loch Doine and Loch Voil, and through Strathyre into Loch Lubnaig, joining the River Teith; and on the north its waters flow into the Dochart, and thence through

FALLS OF CONNEL.

Loch Tay into the River Tay. On the other side of the railway, on a hill to the left, opposite the remains of the Caledonian Forest, there is a stream (which joins the ·Fillan about a mile below Tyndrum) in which a piscatorial curiosity is to be found—the trout there having a projecting underlip, and a sort of pug-nose. We are not aware of any other stream in Scotland in which trout of this peculiar breed is caught, nor does there appear to be any explanation of why there should be · this eccentric formation of fish in that particular burn. The next point of interest is the station of Crianlarich, about nine miles from Ardlui, and about thirty-six and a half from Craigendoran.

Crianlarich—where the traveller, who wishes to break his journey, will find not only unrivalled mountain scenery, but also, what is even more essential in these wilds, a very comfortable hostelry—is the point at which the West Highland Railway, running from south to north, intersects the Callander and Oban Railway, running from east to west, the former line

LOCH TAY.

VIADUCT OF WEST HIGHLAND RAILWAY, CROSSING THE CALLANDER AND OBAN RAILWAY,

crossing the latter on a high viaduct. It is a little village, lying on the ridge that closes Glen Falloch, and it used to be regarded as the limit of civilisation in these parts, the Callander and Oban metals being looked on as the boundary.

All around tower grand eminences, the most notable being Ben More (3,843 feet) and Stobinian (3,827) to the east; both pyramidal mountains with flattened summits, the most lofty by 500 feet that we have yet seen. To the west lie Ben Dhu-Craig (3,204 feet) and Ben Oss (3,374), while in every quarter of the compass rise heights ranging from 2,000 to 3,000 feet. Wherever the eye wanders it is confronted by majestic hills, which seem to crowd and hustle each other

BEN LAWERS, FROM LOCH TAY.

CALLANDER, OFF FOR THE TROSSACHS.

into the narrow valleys, and one is reminded of Rudyard Kipling's little kingdom on the road to Thibet, which was 11,000 feet above the level of the sea and exactly four miles square, "but most of the miles stood on end owing to the nature of the country." If a distribution of three acres and a cow were made, the cottars of such districts as that around Crianlarich would have the best of the bargain, for each man would have to be allotted a mountain with his acres, or a substantial section of one, and would be laird of half a mile of country "stood on end." The principal "lion" of Crianlarich is, of course, Ben More; and the second is Donald Malloch, an ancient and typical Highlander, who seems to be factor, forester, gamekeeper, and various other functionaries on that part of the Breadalbane property, rolled into one. The most interesting feature about this venerable and convivial Gael, is the fact that he can trace his ancestry back three thousand years, to the Prophet Malachi—a matter of distinct historical interest.

At Crianlarich the tourist is presented with as bewildering a series of alternative routes as at Arrochar and Tarbet. He can proceed northwards by the West Highland Railway, which is the course we recommend ; or he can break off here and leave the remainder of the line for the return journey, going west to Oban by the Callander and Oban, thence north-east by Loch Linnhe to Fort William, and back to Crianlarich by the West Highland. If the time at his disposal do not permit of either of these attractive journeys, he can strike west to Oban, as before, passing Dalmally and the Falls of Connel, and there take steamer back to Glasgow by way of Crinan Canal and the Kyles of Bute. If his inclination, on the other hand, be eastward, he can take the Callander and Oban Railway to Killin, sail along Loch Tay to Kenmore, thence coach to Aberfeldy and take train, *via* Perth, to Edinburgh or Glasgow; or from Killin he may go by rail to Lochearnhead, coach alongside Loch Earn to St. Fillans and Comrie, and thence make his way by rail whither he pleases. Finally, he can go round by Callander, come through the Trossachs, thence coach to Aberfoyle and rail to Edinburgh or Glasgow, or sail along Loch Katrine, coach to Stronachlacher, sail to Tarbet and pick up the West Highland Railway at the station there—or sail to Balloch at the southern end of Loch Lomond and thence by rail to Glasgow, reversing the route we sketched from Inversnaid. Each of these alternatives is tempting to the

DALMALLY.

LOOKING UP STRATHFILLAN.

lover of the beautiful and the sublime in Nature; but not one of them will afford him such diversity of striking landscape than the route we have now to follow—north and west to Fort William and back by Glencoe. Wonderful as the scenery has been through which we have already passed, it is only from Crianlarich onwards that the country assumes its finest fascination: the charm of a land hitherto unexplored, a wild and lovely desert in which every frowning peak, every gleaming tarn, every stretch of brilliant moorland is a fresh surprise; a glorious waste where man is a stranger, and where there is nothing to clash with the poetry of the Creator's handiwork.

DUNOLLY CASTLE, OBAN.

From Crianlarich, Strathfillan strikes off to the north-west, and Glen Dochart to the north-east, but the two valleys are really one, which makes a bend at Crianlarich. It is threaded all the way by a single stream, which is called the Fillan at first, and afterwards the Dochart, as it approaches the Loch of that name. The course of the West Highland

BRIDGE OF DOCHART.

Railway is up Strathfillan, running almost parallel with the Callander and Oban for about five miles. The two diverge at Tyndrum, the former going north, and the latter west. After crossing the Fillan, but before Tyndrum Station is reached, two very interesting points are passed, first, the ancient church of St. Fillan, and second, the scene of the famous fight of Dalry. Those who wish to visit these note-worthy points and to see the beauties of great Glen Lyon, should stop a day at Tyndrum, where they will find an exceptionally comfortable hotel. It belongs to the same land-lord as the little hostelry at Crianlarich, but is a much more

REMAINS OF OLD CLACHLAN ON LOCH EARN HEAD.
ONE OF ROB ROY'S HIDING PLACES.

ambitious establishment; and in the proprietor, the traveller will find a type of what a Highland host should be. The reason for the presence of such a large and well-appointed hotel at Tyndrum is that the place is in high favour with mountaineers as a centre and for anglers.

Strathfillan was one of the earliest routes in Scotland along which Christianity made its way; and St. Fillan, one of the first preachers of the Gospel in the north, came down the glen, journeying from Iona, and established here a Culdee

PASS OF BRANDER, LOCH AWE.

church, now known as St. Fillan's Chapel. It lies on the left of the line, about two miles and a half from Crianlarich. The old bell has been taken to Edinburgh, but a still more interesting reminder of the past is the Holy Pool. In this the sick used to be dipped to cure them of their troubles; and a still more curious method was adopted towards the

BEN LEDI, FROM CALLANDER.

mentally diseased. Lunatics used to be brought to the Pool, from far and near, bound hand and foot, and thrown in. At the bottom of the Pool there were a number of large pebbles and if the drowning wretch could

OBAN.

bring up one of these, when he came to the surface, he was regarded as miraculously restored to sanity, and the pebble was added to a cairn on the bank as a memorial. If he failed to bring up the stone, even then the cure of the lunatic was not regarded as absolutely hopeless. He was given another chance—if such a one-sided ordeal can be called a chance for a poor demented creature. He was dragged out of the Pool, and laid on a certain place on the floor of the Chapel, still bound hand and foot. There he was left all night on a slab of stone, half drowned and helpless. If in the morning it was found that he had succeeded in loosing his bonds, then he was proclaimed sane —the devils that possessed him having been driven out by St. Fillan; but if he was discovered in the morning still tied fast, then he was an incurable lunatic. If a person, already deficient in mental balance, were put through the experiences we have related, there would be little doubt, we should imagine, about his lunacy in the morning, if he survived. In this respect the treatment was doubtless successful, that it removed all dubiety, either bringing his madness to a head, or despatching him to his long home. Witches, too, used to be brought to this Holy Pool, and tested in an equally disagreeable way. Their thumbs and great toes were tied together, and they were cast into the water. If in this plight they succeeded in either floating or in scrambling ashore, they were proved witches, and were burned at the stake accordingly; but if they sank, and remained down, then they were innocent; and were probably found to be drowned when dragged out.

About two miles beyond St. Fillan's Chapel, on the same side of the line, by the bank of the stream, is the scene of the Battle of Dalry—inseparably connected in the memory with the name of Robert the Bruce. Having slain his rival, the Red Comyn, before the high altar of the Church of the Minorites, in Dumfries, he was compelled to raise his standard against Edward the First sooner than he had intended. He hastily collected his followers, and was crowned King of Scotland, in the Abbey of Scone, in March 1306; but in June was totally defeated near Methven, in Perthshire. With a few brave adherents, Bruce retreated into the Highlands, where great hardships were suffered, the little band being frequently attacked and driven from one place to another. When he attempted to penetrate into Argyllshire he found the M'Dougals in arms against him, under their chief, John of Lorn, who was

LOCH DOCHART.

a relative of the assassinated Red Comyn. The remainder of the tale may best be told in the words of Sir Walter Scott:—" Bruce was defeated by this chief, through force of

85

numbers, at a place called Dalry ; but he showed, amidst his misfortunes, the greatness of his strength and courage. He directed his men to retreat through a narrow pass, and placing himself last of the party, he fought with, and slew such of the enemy, as attempted to press hard on them. Three followers of M'Dougal, a father and two sons, called M'Androsser, all very strong men, when they saw Bruce thus protecting the retreat of his followers, made a vow that they

BRUCE AND THE BROOCH OF LORN.

FALLS OF CRUACHAN, LOCH AWE.

would either kill this redoubted champion or make him prisoner. The whole three rushed on the King at once. Bruce was on horseback, in the straight pass we have described, betwixt a precipitous rock and a deep lake. He struck the first man, who came up and seized his horse's rein, such a blow with his sword, as cut off his hand and freed the bridle. The man bled to death. The other brother had grasped Bruce in the meantime by the leg and was attempting to throw him from horseback. The King, setting spurs to his horse, made the animal suddenly spring forward, so that the Highlander fell under the horse's feet; and, as he was endeavouring to rise again, Bruce cleft his head in two with his sword. The father, seeing his two sons thus slain, flew desperately at the King, and grasped him by the mantle so close to his body, that he could not have room to wield his long sword. But with the heavy pommel of that weapon, or, as others say, with an iron hammer which hung at his saddle-bow, the King struck this third assailant so heavy a blow that he dashed out his brains. Still, however, the Highlander kept his dying grasp on the King's mantle; so that, to be free of the dead body, Bruce was obliged to undo the brooch, or clasp, by which it was fastened, and leave that, and the mantle itself, behind him. The brooch, which fell thus into the possession of M'Dougal of Lorn, is still preserved in that ancient family, as a memorial that the celebrated Robert Bruce once narrowly escaped falling into the hands of their ancestor." `

In " The Lord of the Isles," also, references will be found to " Teyndrum's dread rout and Methven's flight," the most striking being the boastful song entitled " The Brooch of Lorn," sung by old Ferrand the minstrel :—

> " Whence the brooch of burning gold,
> That clasps the Chieftain's mantle-fold,
> Wrought and chased with fair device,
> Studded fair with gems of price,
> On the varied tartans beaming,
> As, through night's pale rainbow gleaming,
> Fainter now—now seen afar,
> Fitful shines the northern star?

> " Moulded thou for monarch's use,
> By the overweening Bruce,
> When the royal robe he tied,
> O'er a heart of wrath and pride ;
> Thence in triumph wert thou torn,
> By the victor hand of Lorn !

> " When the gem was won and lost,
> Wildly was the war-cry tossed !
> Rung aloud Bendourish fell,
> Answered Douchart's sounding dell ;
> Fled the deer from wild Teyndrum,
> When the homicide o'ercome,
> Hardly 'scaped, with scathe and scorn,
> Left the pledge with conquering Lorn ! "

On an islet on Loch Dochart may yet be seen the ruins of an old castle, where Bruce found refuge at one time during his wanderings between the mountains of Breadalbane and Perthshire and the mountains of Argyllshire. Tradition says he sought asylum there after this battle of Dalry ; but there appears better foundation for the story we have already related—that he retreated down Glen Falloch to " Rob Roy's

Cave " on Loch Lomond.   On the other side of the Fillan, from Dalry, but close at hand, there is a tarn called Loch Nenarm, into which Bruce's followers are said to have thrown their arms, that they might be able to flee the faster from the M'Dougals, who numbered a thousand to their three hundred.

About a mile beyond Dalry, Tyndrum station is reached, four and a half miles from Crianlarich, and forty-one from Craigendoran. On the hill to the left, above the hotel, there used to be lead-mines worked by Lord Breadalbane; they lie about two-thirds up the hill, and never paid owing to the cost of transport.   All the hills in this neighbourhood are rich in lead, and may be opened up now that the railway runs to their base.   About a mile beyond Tyndrum the line crosses the county march between Perthshire and Argyllshire, at an elevation of 1,025 feet.   The boundary is the great watershed of Scotland, and we find the mountain torrents now pouring westward to the Atlantic through Argyllshire, instead of eastward through Perthshire to the German Ocean. The course of the line is along the slopes of wild hills, bare of trees, that would be dark and forbidding but for the

LOCH TULLA AND CRANNOCH WOOD.

warm glow of the heather that clothes their rocky sides, turning the barren wilderness into a blaze of colour. The great bulk of Ben Doran is seen in front, and presently we reach its very foot, after curving round a horse-shoe loop by two viaducts at Auch, which lies at the mouth of Glen Lyon. This is one of the grandest and one of the longest glens in Scotland, stretching right through to Aberfeldy. A coach-road is meditated from the railway to this glen, so that travellers may strike eastward if they wish. The route will be particularly attractive in conjunction with that we are now describing—from Craigendoran, the whole length of the West Highland line to Fort William, back by Ballachulish and Glencoe to Bridge of Orchy, and thence, with only a few miles over the track already followed, eastward through Glen Lyon to Aberfeldy. The natural approach to the Glen is from Auch, the coach-road to follow the shores of Loch Lyon; but the necessities of construction makes the starting-point Gortan, seven and a half miles north-east, as the crow flies, the coach-road passing down Glen Murran to Invermurran, at the foot of the Loch, where the actual Glen would be entered. Between the two routes there is little to choose in point of picturesqueness; but, for the pedestrian, the best approach at present is by way of Tyndrum and Auch.

The railway, on leaving Auch behind, passes round the side of Ben Doran, which towers up on the right to a height of 3,523 feet, in a fine steep slope, the close proximity of this grand mountain being one of the most impressive scenic features yet encountered by the traveller along this ever-varying route. It seems taking a most unwarrantable liberty to cut a railway along the base of a mountain about which Ossian raved, and about which Duncan Ban McIntyre, the last of the great Gaelic bards, composed that grand song, like a march played on the bag-pipes, which Donald Malloch of Crianlarich, the descendant of Malachi the Prophet, can chant so well over a half-mutchkin! On the left the desolate hills of Glen Orchy are seen, branching off to the south-west, wild as a nightmare. At this point, midway between Glen Orchy and Glen Lyon, one remembers with peculiar vividness the words of Scott's "MacGregor's Gathering:"—

> "The moon's on the lake, and the mist's on the brae,
> And the Clan has a name that is nameless by day;
> Then gather, gather, gather, Grigarach!

KILCHURN CASTLE,

LOCH AWE.

G

"Our signal for fight, that from monarchs we drew,
Must be heard but by night in our vengeful haloo!
Then haloo, Grigarach! haloo, Grigarach!

"Glen Orchy's proud mountains, Coalchuirn and her towers
Glenstrae and Glenlyon no longer are ours;
We're landless, landless, landless, Grigarach!"

Glen Orchy leads down to the head of Loch Awe, and it
is by that Loch that Glenstrae lies, and Coalchuirn (or
Kilchurn) Castle. About seven miles and a half from Tyndrum the train reaches Bridge of Orchy.

At this point, some forty-eight and a half miles from Craigendoran, even the coach-road stopped, in the days before the
railway was constructed, and travellers who wished to go
further north had to trust to their own legs or to those of

a hill pony, for the track was little more than a sheep-path. Ever since leaving Crianlarich, some twelve miles back, we have been travelling through a country consecrated to sport, of which fact a significant illustration is to be seen in the little rattling squares of tin hung at intervals along the telegraph wires, and particularly at the openings of glens. These are known as "grouse protectors," and are hung thus in order that their noise in the wind may warn the grouse of the existence of a danger, and prevent them hurling themselves in full flight against the telegraph wires. But although those steep hill slopes, those sunken valleys, and those stretches of barren moorland, have been unbroken by human habitation, save an occasional lonely shieling, and have been peopled only by deer and wildfowl, and the coney that "maketh his dwelling amongst the rocks;" it is only now that we are entering the real home of the wild game, both great and small. For about five-and-twenty miles due north the land is untrodden, except by the sportsman and the shepherd. The last connection with the South breaks off at Bridge of Orchy, the coach-road striking away to the north-west towards Glencoe. Those who wish to see that sublime Glen will find a coach service from Bridge of Orchy, right through to Ballachulish on Loch Leven, whence a steamer will take them north to Fort William, to Inverness by the Caledonian Canal, or south to Oban, by Loch Linnhe. But the most interesting route (which we describe later) is to proceed by the West Highland all the way to Fort William, and return through Glencoe to Bridge of Orchy, thus making a complete

ROB ROY'S PUTTING STONE, GLEN ORCHY.

circuit, then going eastward as already explained, by Glen Lyon, a route to be made shortly practicable by the construction of a coach-road. There is no hotel at Bridge of Orchy, but it is a short run to Tyndrum, where an excellent hotel will be found.

On leaving Bridge of Orchy, the railway follows for a mile and a half the course of the River Orchy, which lies a quarter of a mile to the left. On the moor, between the river and the railway, will be observed a gigantic boulder, weighing some thousands of tons. This is "Rob Roy's Putting Stone," which the mighty MacGregor endeavoured to "put" from the top of Ben Doran across the valley to the hill opposite. For the literal accuracy of this anecdote we do not vouch: we give it as we got it from a simple-hearted native, who was anxious to give us the fullest information about the district. Presently the river is lost in Loch Tulla, a sheet of water about two and a half miles long by three quarters wide, noted for its salmon and trout fishing. The line runs along the Loch side, but at a con-

LOCH TULLA AND ACHALLADER CASTLE.

siderable height above the water, and a fine view is obtained of the great Black Mount deer forest, which the railway skirts for about ten miles. It covers an area of 80,000 acres, stretching as far west as Glen Etive and Glencoe, and is one of the best in Scotland. It belongs to the Marquis of Breadalbane, whose shooting lodge may be seen among the trees on the south-western shore of the Loch. To those unfamiliar with Scotland it will appear to be a misnomer to call this vast area of barren mountains and waste moorlands

a deer forest, for
on it, except in
a few isolated
patches, there seems to grow
nothing higher than heather; but, nevertheless, it is a model of
what a Scottish deer forest should be.

From the north-eastern extremity of the Loch the Water
of Tulla finds exit, the railway continuing to follow the
course of the valley. About a mile beyond the Loch, on
the bank of the Tulla Water, lies a picturesque old ruin,
Achallader Castle, an ancient stronghold of the Fletchers.
Around this lonely keep many a tough fight was fought
some centuries ago, and the graves of the slain are marked
by cairns on the neighbouring heath. Soon after this ruin
is passed the line enters the Crannach Wood, another relic
of the great Caledonian Forest. The wood covers a tract
about a mile square, beginning on the eastern bank of the
Tulla Water and extending up the hillside, so that it lies
both to right and left of the railway. Like the former
remnants of the Caledonian Forest we saw in Glen Falloch,
the trees are grand and aged types of the real Scottish fir,
their great red and grey trunks bent "in a thousand shapes
of resistance and of destruction, their knotted and tortuous
branches stretched out in sturdy and fantastic forms of de-
fiance to the whirlwind and the winter." They are thinly

scattered over the muir and up the hill, the shadow of one hardly reaching to the foot of another, but to look along a vista of such trees as those, the sombre green of their wide-spread branches standing out in strong relief against the background of purple heather and brown mosses on the hill-side, is an experience never forgotten by the artistic mind. It is a picture the composition of which has taken many a century of that infinite care which Nature bestows upon her work.

CRANNACH WOOD, NEAR GORTAN.

ACROSS THE MOOR

A S we emerge from the old Caledonian Forest, we get the first glimpse of Ben Nevis, rearing its snow-clad peak twenty miles to the north-west, but the hills on either hand gradually recede, and instead of threading a narrow glen, we find ourselves traversing an undulating moorland, ever widening and increasing in grandeur. We are entering on the third great section of the journey. During the first, the vast Lochs were all in all; along the second, the majesty of the Mountains overshadowed us; and now comes a striking change, in the shape of the famous Moor of Rannoch. About a mile beyond the Crannach Wood is a passing place called Gortan, whence, according to one scheme, the coach-road for Glen Lyon will diverge to the right, as already explained. The flat country between the Caledonian Forest and Gortan, is called the Crannach Moor, and is not, strictly speaking, part of the great desert we have now to cross; but at Gortan the Moor of Rannoch may be said to begin.

HIGHLAND CATTLE.

Rannoch Moor is the great table-land of Scotland, and even the Moor

TREE ROOTS IN THE PEAT ON RANNOCH MOOR.

RANNOCH MOOR AND MOUNTAINS OF GLENCOE.

of Caithness shrinks into insignificance beside it. It is about twenty miles square, and is surrounded by an amphitheatre of hills, seen dimly in the distance. To say that it is a morass, twenty miles long and twenty miles broad, would convey a mental picture suggesting the most dismal reflections to the traveller who has booked through. We, therefore, hasten to reassure him by asserting emphatically that the Moor of Rannoch is one of the most picturesque stretches on the whole route, and is better described as a wide expanse of moorland, broken up by a multitude of little hillocks and big granite boulders, with peaty tarns and diminutive lochs in the hollows. When an artist, on a sketching

98

tour, reaches the Moor of Rannoch, there he remains until his time is exhausted. Monotonous it certainly is to the pedestrian, who toils over it heavy-footed from Kinloch Rannoch to Kingshouse; but from the window of a railway-carriage it is the reverse of wearisome. There is an infinite solitude in its vast and open expanse, that renders it a spectacle never to be erased from the memory of the dweller in busy cities. An idea of its loneliness and weird uniformity, may, perhaps, best be conveyed by mentioning the fact that in winter it has been no uncommon thing for shepherds to be lost in the snow, and to perish on the Moor for lack of land-marks—those hardy Highland shepherds who know every stone, every bush, every tuft of heather almost, on the miles over which their flocks wander. Macculloch has

SCHEHALLION, FROM RANNOCH MOOR.

described the moor as "a great level, 1,000 feet above the sea, sixteen or twenty miles long, and nearly as much wide, bounded by mountains so distant as scarcely to form an appreciable boundary—open, silent, solitary. Not even the mountain bee was on the wing to give life to the scene; nay, the very midges seemed to scorn the Moor of Rannoch. No water stirred to indicate that something yet lived or moved. The heart-sinking stillness of this solitude was the more dreary that it was so spacious."

This is a very vivid piece of word-painting, from the point of view of a man on foot; but he was unfortunate in the season of his visit as regards insect-life. Why, the whole

ENTRANCE TO GLEN ORCHY.

moor in summer is a-buzz with bees; there are midges in plenty, if they can be taken as any amelioration of the dreariness of the waste, and there are burns where the dark brown dappled beauty of the burn trout is well known to the skilful angler. Moreover, it is, perhaps, the finest grouse-moor in Scotland, and it is over-run, particularly towards the hills, with the white hare. During the construction of the railway, a party of five guns in a day's shooting bagged 150 hares, an average of thirty to the gun. Among those who have not seen the moor, the impression is that it is as flat as the face of a loch, but this is by no means so. It is full of undulations and little

LOCH LYDOCH, RANNOCH MOOR.

knolls, and it is the complete absence of tree and shrub that invests it with such utter nakedness. The surface is the most treacherous walking imaginable, the bog being broken throughout into tufts of sod, separated by peat "hags"—shallow black ditches, meandering hither and thither, and forming a maze of slippery snares for the pedestrian, at every few yards. In winter the moor is simply twenty miles square of a study in sepia ; but in summer the brilliance of the colouring is marvellous. The purple heather, the green mosses, the yellow grasses, and the rich·brown of the peat hags, with here and there the delicate azure of the harebell—by itself, all but unseen—combine to form a luminous mass of lovely tints. The whole moor appears to be covered with one colossal Turkey carpet, so rich and oriental is the colouring.

All around in the peat hags, projecting from the sides of

MARMORE DEER FOREST, FROM RANNOCH MOOR.

the rent moss, are to be seen the brown contorted roots of enormous trees, with here and there a splintered section of a huge trunk, giving unmistakeable evidence that this unclad waste was once covered by a mighty race of trees, the ancient Caledonian Forest, whose survivors we have seen. Wherever a cutting is made on Rannoch Moor, there roots and stumps of giant firs are found ; and it is curious to learn, that although the wood may have been buried in the soaking moss for a thousand years, it burns like a torch. Not only has the bed of peat preserved it from decay, but the old pine roots retain their resin and oils. It is not very many years since these ancient roots were the favourite means of illumination in the shielings of the district. We know of an old shepherd and his wife who used to live in a hut towards Kingshouse, on the western verge of Rannoch Moor, who unwillingly abandoned the use of this primitive lamp in favour of paraffin only about five years ago. When he had gathered his flock into the fold, the shepherd would

BURNING FIR ROOTS, RANNOCH.

return to his low thatch-covered shieling with an armful of the roots, to be dried before the great peat fire for a night. In the morning he would break them into small pieces, about the size of a finger, and in the dark winter evenings it was the duty of the old man to keep one of the little torches flaring while his aged wife sat spinning at her wheel in the "ingle-neuk." The method of burning the roots was curious. From the crook in the chimney hung an iron instrument, like the "girdle" on which oat-cakes are baked, but instead of presenting to the fire a flat surface, the "girdle" was ribbed with bars like a gridiron. One of the small pieces of resinous fir-root was placed on these bars and blazed up in the heat of the fire, illuminating the whole hut, and as soon as the flare began to die out the old shepherd would put on another, the whirr of the spinning-wheel never ceasing. Such a spectacle as this was to be seen until quite recently in hundreds of shielings around the moor.

Even if the traveller be inclined to regard the Moor of Rannoch as dismal, the landscape will assume a new interest in his eyes when he is reminded that it is the scene of some of the most exciting episodes in that heart-stirring book of Robert Louis Stevenson's, "Kidnapped," one of the finest pieces of word-painting, and character sketching, published since the death of Scott. No man has a right to claim knowledge of contemporary literature unless he is thoroughly familiar with "Kidnapped." Those who furbish up their memories will remember that the wild Jacobite Highlander, Alan Breck, and the hero, young David Balfour of Shaws, fled for their lives, in the year 1751, from the shores of Loch Leven, pursued by the revengeful Campbells, who thought them guilty of the famous Appin murder (of which we have more to say at a later stage). From Duror, in Appin, they made their way along the southern boundary of Glencoe, crossed that Glen, and after considerable suffering made their way along the northern boundary to the point where the mountains sink into this great plain, at the opening of Glen Etive. "More than eleven hours of incessant hard travelling brought us, early in the morning, to the end of a range of mountains. In front of us there lay a piece of low, broken, desert land, which we must now cross. The sun was not long up, and shone straight in our eyes; a little thin mist went up in the face of the moorland like a smoke, so that (as Alan said) there might have been twenty squadron of dragoons there and we none the wiser." They debate as to the path to be taken, discarding north and south for good

reasons. "'Well, then, east, ye see, we have the muirs,' said
Alan. 'Once there, David, its mere pitch-and-toss. Out on
yon bald, naked, flat place, where can a body turn to? Let
the red-coats come over a hill, they can spy you miles away;
and the sorrow's in their horse's heels they would soon ride
you down. It's no good place, David; and I'm free to say,
it's worse by day-light than by dark.'" In the preface,
Mr. Stevenson makes apology for several geographical and
historical liberties he has taken, but he does not include
amongst them the suggestion of cavalry making headway
across Rannoch Moor. According to our observation, there
is not an acre of the moor over which a dragoon could
gallop, or indeed walk his horse. Even a stag would have
to pick his way very gingerly, and we never saw one try.
We point this out without any reflection on the merit of the
story, for a novelist is allowed a little license as well as a poet.

The passages describing their flight over the moor are so
vivid, and will appeal so strongly to the traveller over the
very scene, that we give a couple of graphic extracts: "The
mist rose and died away, and showed us that country lying
as waste as the sea; only the moor-fowl and the peewits
crying upon it, and far over to the east, a herd of deer,

moving like dots. Much of it was red with heather; much of the rest broken up with bogs and hags and peaty pools; some had been burnt black in a heath fire; and in another place there was quite a forest of dead firs, standing like skeletons A wearier looking desert man never saw, but at least it was clear of troops, which was our point. We went down accordingly into the waste, and began to make our toilsome and devious travel towards the eastern verge. There were the tops of mountains all round (you are to remember) from whence we might be spied at any moment; so it behoved us to keep in the hollow parts of the moor, and when these turned aside from our direction, to move upon its naked face with infinite care. Sometimes, for half an hour together, we must crawl from one heather bush to another, as hunters do when they are hard upon the deer. It was a clear day again, with a blazing sun; the water in the brandy-bottle was soon gone; and altogether if I had guessed what it would be to crawl half the time upon my belly and to walk much of the rest stooping nearly to the knees, I should certainly have held back from such a killing enterprise. Toiling and resting, and toiling again, we wore away the morning; and about noon lay down in a thick bush of heather to sleep."

Overcome with weariness, David Balfour falls asleep when it is his turn to watch, and when he awakes the sun is up and—"A body of horse-soldiers had come down during my sleep, and were drawing near to us from the south-east, spread out in the shape of a fan, and riding their horses to and fro in the deep parts of the heather" Stevenson insists on putting his dragoons on Rannoch Moor! The case is a desperate one, for if they are caught they are both dead men, and Alan at once recommences the flight for life :—
"He began to run forward on his hands and knees with an incredible quickness, as though it were his natural way of going. All the same, too, he kept winding in and out in the lower parts of the moorland, where we were the best concealed. Some of these had been burned, or at least scathed with fire; and there arose in our faces (which were close to the ground) a blinding, choking dust, as fine as smoke.

The water was long out; and this posture of running on the hands and knees brings an overmastering weakness and weariness, so that the joints ache, and the wrists faint, under your weight. Now and then, indeed, where was a big bush of heather, we lay awhile and panted, and putting aside the leaves, looked back at the dragoons. They had not spied us, for they held straight on; a-half troop, I think, covering about two miles of ground, and beating it mighty thoroughly as they went. I had awakened just in time: a little later, and we must have fled in front of them, instead of escaping

GAUER WATER, RANNOCH.

on one side. Even as it was, the least misfortune might betray us;- and now and again, when a grouse rose out of the heather with a clap of wings, we lay as still as the dead, and were afraid to breathe."

By dint of such desperate efforts, Alan and David escape the soldiers, and reach the safe shelter of Ben Alder, which lies on the north-eastern verge of the Moor, by the side of Loch Ericht—a mountain we shall see presently. Thence they eventually make their way south, across Loch Rannoch, and through Glen Murran, where some of their worst sufferings are experienced, to Glen Lyon. This brings us back to Gortan, from which Glen Murran strikes off to the south-east, and where the moor begins.

At Gortan, then, we enter Rannoch Moor, and proceed through the. midst of that silent waste, which stretches for miles and miles to the right and left, until its dazzling colours die into the brown distance, and at last merge in the blue of the far-away hills surrounding the desert. To travel over this section by day is a memorable experience, but best of all it is to cross the moor in the evening, for the sunsets on that desolate moss are incredibly beautiful As the sun sinks behind the distant western peaks it turns them to gold, while their shoulders darken into a profound blue, like the blue of mid-ocean, and the level rays of the dying orb pour over the vast plain in broad pathways of light, shedding a new glory on the sodden moss and turning the dark peat-hags into streaks of silver, around which the heather and clusters of wild flowers spring up like flames of fire. The sun dips behind the mountain-tops leaving only a radiance in the sky, and a grey veil seems to descend on the moor, fold by fold, dimming the bright hues of the barren heath until all around lies a dreary brown expanse, like the Saragossa sea, tossing its matted weed in hillocks after a storm ; while on the west, some distant glen lies, like a Land of Goshen, in a very noon-tide of sunlight. Those who wish to know this wonderful moor, as it should be known, must so time their journeys that either the first visit or the return is in the evening. To see a sunset on Rannoch Moor is as essential as to see Loch Lomond by moonlight.

Rannoch Moor used to be regarded as an impass-able barrier by railway engineers. Several schemes were mooted in the past, but they always broke down at Rannoch Moor. As now constructed, the West Highland Railway virtually floats over the moor. The moor was deep and cross-drained to take off the water, and across the trenches was laid a thick layer of brushwood. On this elastic founda-tion the permanent way was laid, making one of the most satisfactory stretches on the line. Instead of the brushwood decaying in the wet peat, as one might be inclined to think, it is pickled and preserved like the roots of the old pine trees which we have described. Maybe a thousand years hence, if excavations are made, the brushwood will be found as fresh as the day it was deposited. There is no question that the line has been well engineered When Mr. Charles Forman, whose scheme it is, had laid down his route from Craigendoran to Fort William, he was astonished to discover in some old Parliamentary papers that an almost identical course, for a turnpike road, had been traced in the beginning of the century by Telford, the famous engineer who constructed the Caledonian Canal. In one sense it was a curious co-incidence, but more properly it might be said to be a voucher for the soundness of the plan, since two engineers had arrived independently at the same conclusions at different dates.

Near Gortan, the county march, between Argyllshire and Perthshire, is again crossed, and for a few miles the railway runs in the latter county again. The watershed is once more traversed, and the streams are now found flowing east to the German Ocean The Tulla Water on the left is followed for some way, and then the Blackwater is taken up on the same side—both narrow streams winding through the irregular surface of the moor Near the bridge over the Blackwater are seen, on both sides of the line, the "Soldiers' Trenches," long parallels cut through the moss and rapidly filling up with the spongy peat These are a relic of the '45, having been cut by the Duke of Cumberland's men after the Jacobite rising. A body of English troops was posted at Rannoch, where the barracks are still to be seen near the Loch, to keep the Highlanders of the district in order. Finding time hanging heavily on the men's hands, their commander set them to the task of digging these trenches, which were absolutely useless for any defensive purpose, as they could be turned on either flank, lying as they did right in the middle of the waste. The railway, which has made a bend to the east, now runs north to the Gauer Water, a swift stream flowing between Loch Lydoch on the left and Loch Rannoch on the right; crossing the stream a mile east of the foot of Loch Lydoch, and reaching Rannoch Station, fifteen and a half miles from Bridge of Orchy, and about sixty-four miles from Craigendoran. Rannoch cannot well claim to be populous, although at the head of Loch Rannoch, seven miles away, there are a number of houses, and along its sides there is a considerable crofting population. Kinloch Rannoch, on the eastern end of the Loch, is a favourite summer resort, notwithstanding the difficulties of its approach which have had hitherto to be encountered. There is a geographical amenity about the place, however, for it is to be the starting point of a coach road along the Gauer and the north side of Loch Rannoch to Struan on the Highland Railway, thus making a

GAUER WATER, SCHEHALLION IN DISTANCE.

very useful connection for the traveller to the Braemar Highlands and the northern counties.

On leaving Rannoch we have a fine view along Loch Lydoch, a narrow sheet of water about five miles long, inclining to the south-west, the brilliant blue of its waters making a beautiful picture amid the surrounding bloom of the heather. The railway now makes a sharp bend to the north-west and skirts Cruach Hill, from which point, owing to the high elevation and the open view, one of the most magnificent prospects on the whole route is obtained. On the left, Loch Lydoch extends into the heart of the Black Mount, where the great hills rise in bold and precipitous

GLEN OGLE.

crags, looming dark against the sky, while further west, tower the mountains of Glen Etive and Glencoe—a mighty and turbulent sea of hills. Far away, in the north-west, are clustered the peaks of Lochaber, with the huge summit of Ben Nevis soaring over all. On the right, to the south-east, are grouped the gloomy mountains of Glen Lyon ; further east may be descried, in the distance, the huge bulk of Schehallion, and north-east opens Glen Ericht, looked down upon by great Ben Alder. In whichever direction the eye be cast it is confronted by a colossal barrier of rock, heaving up into the sky in a thousand impressive outlines.

Towards Ben Alder the traveller will turn with peculiar interest, for it was on that "wild desert mountain, full of hills and hollows," which rises to a height of 3,757 feet, that the heroes of "Kidnapped" found safety on their escape from the moor. On the southern flank of "that dismal mountain of Ben Alder" lies what is known as "Prince Charlie's Cave," where the Young Pretender lay hid with Cluny Macpherson and Lochiel, after the disastrous battle of Culloden. This was one of the refuges in which Cluny, the Chief of the Clan Macpherson, lived for about nine years after that battle, safe in the fidelity of his people, although his country was over-run by troops who would have gone to any pains to capture this Jacobite leader, had they known of his proximity. Under the name of "Cluny's Cage," a very good description of this curious lair is given by Stevenson, when Alan Breck and David Balfour seek asylum there with Cluny Macpherson :—"We came at last to the foot of an exceeding steep wood, which scrambled up a craggy hillside, and was crowned by a naked precipice The trees clung upon the slope, like sailors on the shrouds of a ship, and their trunks were like the rounds of a ladder, by which we mounted. Quite at the top, and just before the rocky face of the cliff sprang above the foliage, we found that strange house, which was known in the country as "Cluny's Cage" The trunks of several trees had been wattled across, the intervals strengthened with stakes, and the ground behind this barricade levelled up with earth to make the floor. A tree, which grew out from the hillside, was the living centre-beam of the roof. The walls were of wattle and covered with moss. The whole house had something of an egg-shape; and it half hung, half stood, in that steep, hillside thicket, like a wasp's nest in a green hawthorn. Within, it was large enough to shelter five or six persons with some comfort. A projection of the cliff had been cunningly employed to be the fireplace, and the smoke rising against the face of the rock, and being not dissimilar in colour, readily escaped notice from below."

South of Ben Alder lies Loch Ericht, which Christopher North describes as "the dreariest, most desolate, and dismal of the' Highland Lochs," and the distance from the West Highland Railway, up Glen Ericht to Dalwhinnie, on the Highland Railway, is seventeen and a half miles, this being the nearest point of approach between the two railways.

Skirting, on the left, the rocky eminences known as the Black Corries, the line passes close, on the same side, a tarn called Loch-na-Chlaidheimh, which is a point of considerable interest. The name is pronounced Loch-na-Clive, the last syllable being apparently unnecessary, but Gaelic is a peculiar language ; for instance, what we pronounce Ben Venue is written in Gaelic, Beinn Mheadhonaidh. The Loch is the

most easterly of a chain of small lakes, joined first by the
Blackwater (not the stream of the same name we crossed
before) and afterwards by the River Leven, which stretch
from east to west, to the head of Loch Leven—an arm of
Loch Linnhe. In the centre of Loch-na-Chlaidheimh three
counties meet — Inverness-shire, Perthshire and Argyllshire,
and thereby hangs a tale. The name means "the Loch of
the Swords," and the story is this :—Late in the fifteenth
century, Lochiel, the Chief of the Camerons, and the Earl
of Atholl, the head of the Atholl family, agreed to
meet alone by this Loch and settle certain boundary disputes. As Lochiel was on his way to the place of appoint-
ment, he was met by an old woman, who stopped the Chief
on the moor with the significant question, "Where are your
men, Lochiel?" The Chief laughed, but the old woman
kept her blear eyes fixed steadily on his face, and croaked
out again, "Where are your men, Lochiel?" "Peace, old
witch!" said Lochiel; "what need have I of a following? I
go to meet only Atholl," and he strode off. But the
uncanny old woman hobbled after him, caught him by the
streaming end of his cloak, and muttered again, with strange
persistence, "Where are your men, Lochiel?" The Chief
could not help feeling uneasy at this obstinate prediction of
evil, and gave way, returning to the nearest clachan and
collecting a "tail" of sixty-five men, who followed him stealthily
and secreted themselves among the heather by the loch-side.
Presently the Earl of Atholl was seen approaching alone, and
Lochiel felt ashamed of his ambush. The two Chiefs met,
and soon came to high words, whereupon the Earl waved
his hand and twenty Atholl Highlanders sprang up from
the heather, where they had been posted in advance. "Who
are these?" said Lochiel. "Atholl wethers," replied the
Earl, significantly, "come to graze on Lochaber pastures."
Lochiel had arranged that if he turned his cloak so as to
present the red side outwards, it was a signal for his men
to show themselves; this he now did, and instantly his
three score and five warriors came bounding down the grassy
steep. Atholl started, and "Who are these?" said he.
"Lochaber dogs," replied Lochiel, "sharp toothed and hungry,

and, oh! so keen to taste the flesh of your Atholl wethers.
Give up, Lord Earl, your claim to these lands, for my dogs are
fierce and cannot much longer be held in leash." Peaceful
negotiations then ensued, and the Earl of Atholl, drawing his
sword and kissing it, renounced his claim "through summer's
heat and winter's cold"; and, sweeping his sword round his

head, tossed it into the lake, proclaiming that the land should
be Lochiel's till the sword was found.

Singularly enough, in 1826, a boy fishing in the Loch,
brought a basket-hilted sword to land, and took it to the
minister of the parish, but so alarmed were the Lochaber men
on hearing of the discovery that they demanded its restoration,
and it was again thrown into the Loch.

At the "Sword Loch" the railway enters Inverness-shire, in
which county it remains until the terminus at Fort William
is reached. To the north-west of the bare little Loch rises

the commanding eminence of Ben-na-Vreich, jutting out as the sharp separation of two valleys. On the left of the railway the Blackwater valley stretches due west to Loch Leven, while on the right the valley of the Tay opens eastward, with proud Schehallion in the distance. A little further on, to the left, about two and a half miles distant to the north-east, a large house is seen, across the moor, and half way up the hill. This is Corrour Lodge, the highest shooting lodge in Scotland, being 1,723 feet above the sea level. It is the property of Sir John Stirling Maxwell, of Pollock; and, according to the omniscient Baddeley, "it disputes with the 'Cat and Fiddle,' near Buxton, the claim to the highest position of any habitation in the kingdom." It lies in the deer forest of Corrour, which we follow on the right, the forest of Ben-na-Vreich lying on the left. About three miles beyond Corrour Lodge, Loch Ossian is passed, a lonely tarn

LOCH OSSIAN.

about four miles long, noted for its splendid trout, and is the highest Loch of any size in Scotland, its elevation above the sea level being 1,269 feet. Opposite this Loch is the passing place of Luibruaridh (pronounced Lebruary), which is at once the termination of Rannoch Moor and the highest point on the line, being 1,350 feet above the sea. A fine view may be obtained, from this point, of Ben Nevis, which lies about twelve miles to the north-west, towering above the hills around it as the dome of St. Paul's towers above the highest roofs of London.

RANNOCH MOOR is now left behind, and a new phase of scenery develops as the line, which has been running north-west from Rannoch to Corrour, strikes due north, and begins to descend into the Spean Valley. Christopher North, whose vigorous remarks on Highland scenery we have frequently quoted, speaks of "a prodigious wilderness, with which perhaps no man alive is conversant, and in which you may travel for days without seeing even any symptoms of human life—the regions comprehended between the Forest of Atholl and Ben Nevis, the Moor of Rannoch and Glen Spean. There are many lochs, and Loch

A BIT OF GLEN NEVIS.

115

Ericht is their griesly Queen. Herdsmen, shepherds, hunters, fowlers, anglers, traverse its borders, but few have been far in the interior, and we never knew anybody who had crossed it from south to north, from east to west." Now, the West Highland Railway traverses it from south to north and from east to west, and the most frail invalid may inspect, at his ease, this prodigious wilderness, which even the Professor, with his mighty and untiring stride, never covered. But the association in one sentence of Rannoch Moor and Glen Spean must not mislead the reader of the "Recreations of Christopher North" into the idea that the two stretches of country are similar in aspect. They are totally distinct; the barren moorland is left behind at Luibruaridh and succeeded by a rugged and romantic country, possessing some of the most picturesque features on the whole hundred-mile run.

Soon after leaving Luibruaridh, Loch Treig comes into view on the left, lying within a stone's throw of the line, but 415 feet below, the railway being cut high in the hillside that overshadows it. Loch Treig is a most striking sheet of water, about five miles and a half in length, and about half a mile in width (at the head) which is first seen from the railway and gradually narrowing to the foot, while

BEN VREICH, FROM LUIBRUARIDH.

116

the line, winding down the shoulder of the hill on a steep
gradient, finishes almost level with the water. On both sides
of the Loch precipitous hills rise sheer from the lake, the
banks being shelving rock. Some years ago, a boat con-
taining two Highlanders capsized at the edge of the Loch,
and one of the men was drowned. When the survivor was
asked to explain how it happened he made the following
perspicuous statement: "Well, sir, you will see, when the boat
did turn over, Tonald and me went down into the water.

LOCH TREIG, LOOKING TOWARDS INVERLAIR.

Loch Treig, as you will know, is a very steep loch, and she
herself will have taken the right turning and will have climbed
out of the water; but Tonald will have taken the wrong turning and climbed down and been trownded." Loch Treig is
famous for its trout, the fish ranging as high as nine pounds,
while twenty pounds is spoken of in the district as a fair
day's basket. As the line dips to the foot of the Loch, a
tiny islet is descried, bearing a few trees. This is "Council
Island," where the chiefs of the Clan Cameron, and the Clan
MacIntosh, used to confer when disputes arose between the
two clans, and it was a question of peace or war. This little
island was selected as the place of meeting in order that the
two chiefs might be safe from such treacherous ambushes
on either side as we described at the "Sword Loch." It had
the additional advantage of being small and in deep water,

HEAD OF LOCH TREIG.

so that if the two chiefs failed to come to an agreement, one of them was likely to go over, and the dispute thus be settled by the silence of one party, and the feud started on a satisfactory basis. On the hillside, overhanging the line, is a huge boulder called the "Watch-Rock," on which the Highland sentinels used to stand to survey the surrounding country when the inroad of a rival clan was expected.

From the foot of Loch Treig pours the river Treig, gradually narrowing as it approaches the Spean, which it enters at Inverlair, after a furious passage down the moorland slopes in a series of foaming rapids. At Inverlair there is a station of the West Highland Railway, seventeen miles from Rannoch, and about eighty-one from Craigendoran. From this point a coach-road strikes off to the north-east, through the Laggan district, along Spean-side and Loch Laggan, to Kingussie (pronounced King-yewsie), on the Highland Railway, whence the Braemar and Aberdeenshire Highlands may be reached.

The only two Gaelic poems extant, subsequent to the Ossianic era, and prior to the sixteenth century—"The Aged Bard's Desire" and "The Owl"—were composed by hunter bards who drew their inspiration from the beautiful mountains which overhang Loch Treig. The former, an exquisite poem, suggests

ON THE SPEAN NEAR
INVERLAIR.

a period before the introduction of Christianity. We pass
Beinn a Bhric (the dappled mountain), where the weird witch
jealously herds her flock of dun deer, and protects them from
the hunter. The spirit of the beautiful and plaintive song which
she is said to sing, "Cailleach Beinn a Bhric," is well rendered
by the Professor of Poetry at Oxford, thus:—

CAILLEACH BEINN A BHRIC.

"Weird wife of Beinn-y-Vreich ! horo ! horo !
  Aloft in the mist she dwells;
Vreich horo ! Vreich horo ! Vreich horo !
  All alone by the lofty wells.

"Weird, weird wife ! with the long grey locks,
  She follows her fleet-foot stags,
Noisily moving through splintered rocks,
  And crashing the grisly crags.

> " Tall wife ! with the long grey hose, in haste
>   The rough strong beach she walks ;
>   But dulse or seaweed she will not taste,
>   Nor yet the green kail stalks.
>
> " 'And I will not let my herds of deer,
>   My bonny red deer, go down ;
>   I will not let them down to the shore,
>   To feed on the sea shells brown.
>
> " 'O, better they love in the Corrie's recess,
>   Or on mountain top to dwell,
>   And feed by my side on the green green cress,
>   That grows by the lofty well.
>
> " 'Broad Beinn-y-Vreich is grisly and drear,
>   But wherever my feet have been,
>   The well springs start for my darling deer,
>   And the grass grows tender and green.' "

At Inverlair, the West Highland Railway changes its course. Hitherto, although with various bends to the east or west, necessitated by the nature of the country (for it is a land in which the towns will have to come to the railway, as there are no towns to which the railway can go), has been making due north, for the difference of longitude between Craigendoran and Inverlair is very minute But now the railway turns due west, crossing the Spean and following its course along the Glen on the northern bank, penetrating the famous Braes of Lochaber. The mention of the name at once brings to mind memories of that wailing Highland lament, "Farewell to Lochaber," which sounded so eerily on the pipes that it had to be forbidden during the Peninsular War on account of its depressing effect on the spirits of the troops. Allan Ramsay's setting of words begins :—

> " Farewell to Lochaber, farewell to my Jean,
>   Where heartsome wi' thee I ha'e mony a day been ;
>   To Lochaber no more, to Lochaber no more,
>   We'll maybe return to Lochaber no more.
>   These tears that I shed, they're a' for my dear,
>   And no for the dangers attending on weir ;
>   Though borne on rough seas to a far bloody shore,
>   Maybe to return to Lochaber no more." .

The speaker is, of course, supposed to be a Highland soldier, embarking for a war in a foreign land.

From Loch Laggan the river Spean pours in a swift torrent, carrying a very heavy volume of water compressed within a narrow channel, which it has cut for itself deep in the hard schist. The railway follows closely the north bank of the ravine down which the fierce current tears its way, the train sometimes appearing to overhang the turbulent stream. The river is a succession of furious cataracts, one of the most striking being seen just after leaving Inverlair. The water thunders down a series of wide steps against a wall of rock so adamantine that the stream swerves at a sharp angle and rushes in a long race of white spume through a straight chute, cut in the black rock as if with the chisel. A little further and we pass, on the right, a village called Achluachrach (a striking name for a Cockney suburban villa), where there is an interesting old burying-ground called St. Cyril. About this ancient God's Acre a quaint anecdote is told by the late Mrs. MacKellar. "Once upon a time a Protestant was buried in this consecrated ground, and forthwith there was a rebellion among the dwellers in those tombs. Night after night the inhabitants of the surrounding districts were disturbed with the shouts of warriors engaged in battle, and the clashing of weapons. At last it came to be unendurable, and a deputation waited on Dr. Ross, the

OLD CALEDONIAN FOREST, BETWEEN BRIDGE OF ORCHY AND GORTAN.

minister of the parish, saying, even though this parishioner of his had been a good man and a friend to the district, yet that he must be removed, or else the dead would never sleep in peace. 'I am not going to remove him ; why don't they turn him out when they're at it ? ' said Dr. Ross ; 'if he had twenty of his own kind with him they would clear the whole churchyard.' The matter, however, came to a crisis on a very stormy night. Women and children sat by the fire in their huts, cowering in fear. One good man at last resolved to venture out and go for the priest, which he did. The priest readily agreed to accompany him, and at a stream he put off a shoe and prepared some holy water in it, with which he proceeded alone to where the Braes men, fierce and furious, were in vain endeavouring to oust this disturber of their rest." The moment the priest had reconsecrated the ground the tumult ceased, and it was never afterwards renewed.

On the hills to the right there has been visible, from Inverlair to this point, one of the mysterious Parallel Roads of Lochaber, which were for so many years a source of sore perplexity among men of science. Of these strange Parallel Roads we shall have more to say when we reach Glen Roy, where the most wonderful examples are found. As we advance along the Spean the valley narrows until it becomes little more than a ravine, and at Monessie Gorge the waterfalls are striking in the extreme. The gorge is narrow and deep, dark crags, fringed with trees, shutting in the rushing torrent, which seethes in thunder and foam down the steep and rocky channel, leaping over the obstructing boulders in clouds of spray that beat on the carriage windows when the stream is in spate, for the train runs on the absolute verge of the cataract, separated from the roaring currrent only by a low parapet. No spectacle on the line more forcibly impresses the memory than these Monessie Falls, the steep black rocks, the dark green foliage at the waters edge, and the white torrent boiling down the rugged bed in a mad delirious ferment, forming a picture that seems an embodiment of the spirit of the Highlands, proud, turbulent and untameable.

A little beyond Monessie, the train stops at Roy Bridge station, about five miles and a half from Inverlair. Here the railway crosses the River Roy, which comes down from Glen Roy, where the Parallel Roads are to be seen. No one should visit this district without inspecting these geological wonders, either by making a trip to the Glen from Fort William, about twelve miles distant, or breaking the journey for the purpose at Roy Bridge, where a hotel will be found. On a clear day a glimpse of the Roads may be had from the train; but to study these natural phenomena it is necessary to walk or drive a few miles up the Glen.

These Parallel Roads have caused one of the keenest scientific controversies of the century, and although their

PARALLEL ROADS OF GLEN ROY.

mystery is now solved, they are still regarded as one of the most unique features in the geological aspect of the country; while even to the non-scientific observer they are full of strange interest. Glen Roy is a gloomy ravine, both long and deep, but less than half a mile wide, shut in on both sides by steep mountain slopes, along whose bases the valley winds its way. Standing at the mouth of the Glen, the observer is amazed to see three distinct horizontal lines running along the eastern hillsides—exactly parallel—the two upper lines far up the hills and separated by about eighty feet, while the lower lies about 200 feet further down the slope. On looking to the western hillsides, he is still more startled to see three exactly similar lines running along the Glen on that side also, not only parallel to each other, but parallel to those on the east, and at precisely the same elevations, the lines following each other for about eight miles. "The long, deep Glen lies before him, with its three bars, straight and distinct, as if they had been drawn with a ruler, yet winding into all the recesses of the steep slopes, and coming out again, over the projecting parts, without ever deviating from their parallelism." His astonishment is increased when, on close inspection, he finds that each of these lines is a level terrace, cut in the face of the hills, and ranging in places over sixty feet in width. How these terraces were cut used to be a problem puzzled over as much by the scientist as by the layman. The Highlanders said they were hunting-walks cut by the Picts for their kings, who used to hold court at Inverlochy Castle, beside Fort William; but this was obviously absurd. The pseudo-scientific visitor said the Roads must have been cut by glaciers at different periods, although they do not show the slightest evidence of glacial action. The truth, as at last discovered, is, that the terraces mark the successive levels of a great loch, "The shores, as it were, of a phantom lake, that came into being with the growth of the glaciers, and vanished as these melted away." That this wide-mouthed glen, opening into another glen, the valley of the Spean, should have been filled with a lake in days gone by seems incredible, but so it was.

 · The story is told briefly and clearly by Professor Geikie in his book on "The Scenery of Scotland," where much may be learned on the geological history of scenery. We quote the gist of the passage in which he explains these Parallel Roads. "Each of them is a shelf or terrace cut by the shore waters of a lake that once filled Glen Roy. The highest is of course the oldest, and those beneath it were formed in succession, as the waters of the lake sank. Until Agassiz suggested the idea of a dam of glacier-ice, the great difficulty in the way of understanding how a lake could ever have filled these valleys was the entire absence of any relic of the barrier that must have kept back the water. The valley of the Caledonian Canal seems to have been filled to the brim with ice, which, choking up the mouths of Glen Gluoy and Glen Spean, served to pond back the waters of these glens. The Glen Treig glacier, in like manner, stretched right across Glen Spean and mounted its north bank. When the lake that must thus have filled Glen Roy and the neighbouring valleys was at its deepest, its surplus waters would

ON THE SPEAN.

escape from the head of Glen Roy down into Strath Spey, and at that time the uppermost beach or parallel road (1,155 feet above the present sea level) was formed. The Glen Treig glacier then shrank a little, and the lake was thus lowered about 78 feet, so as to form the middle terrace, which is 1,077 feet above the sea, the outflow being now by the head of Glen Glaster (*Gleann glas dhoire*) and through Loch Laggan into the Spey. After the lake had remained for a time at that height, the Glen Treig glacier continued on the

SPEAN BRIDGE.

decline, and at last crept out of Glen Spean. By this means the level of the lake was reduced to 862 feet above the sea, and the waters of Glen Roy joined those of Loch Laggan, forming one long winding lake, having its outflow, by what is now the head of Glen Spean, into Strath Spey. · While this level was maintained the lowest of the parallel roads of Glen Roy was formed. As the climate grew milder, however, the mass of ice which choked up the mouth of Glen Spean, and ponded back the water, gradually melted away. The drainage of Glen Roy, Glen Spean and their tributary valleys was then no longer arrested, and as the lake sank in level, the streams one by one took their places in the channels which they have been busy widening and deepening ever since" In confirmation of this theory, the lower of the three Parallel Roads may be traced along Glen Spean.

At Roy Bridge, on the left, is Keppoch House, the ancient seat of the MacDonells of Keppoch. This was the scene of the "Keppoch Murder," so terribly avenged, which took place in 1663. The chieftain of the MacDonells of Keppoch had died, leaving two young sons, who were being educated in France On their father's death the lads came home, and invited their uncle's seven sons to dine with them. These surly youths, jealous of the succession to power of their two cousins, picked a quarrel with them over their French manners, slew them with their dirks, and seized the inheritance. Old Ian Lom, the Keppoch bard, on discovering what had happened, set out north for Invergarry, on the bank of Loch Oich, through which the Caledonian Canal now runs. Having reached the Castle he demanded of Lord Macdonnell and Aross, the chief of the clan, revenge against the murderers of his kinsmen. The chief gave him fifty men, with whom the bard returned to Keppoch, seized the house, slew the seven brothers, and cut off their heads. He then set out again for Invergarry, carrying the heads on his back, bound together by a heather-rope through their hair. "He went with them, glad as a farmer carrying golden sheaves, and laid them down at the feet of Glengarry, after washing them in the well of the seven heads that stands on the banks of Loch Oich." ·The name of this

well is Tober-na'n-Ceann, which means "the well of the heads."
Over the well there is now a monument, surmounted by seven
heads in stone.

At Inverlair, in the lifetime of Captain Alexander
Macdonald, 82nd Regiment (a brother officer of Sir John
Moore), the last resting place was opened of those who suffered
in this tragedy. The early part of this century was the age
of scepticism in the veracity of Celtic song and tradition; but
the number and position of the headless bodies, confirmed in
every particular the account given in the poem of the bard
"Ian Lom." The tombstone of the revengeful old bard, who
was the last Celtic poet-laureate (to Charles II.), may be seen

BHEIN VHAN, FROM GLEN ROY.

through the trees on the summit of St. Cyril's cemetery as we
pass beneath. The ruined chapel close by is one of the seven
penitentiary churches built by "Allein nan Creagh" (Allan of
the Forays), a turbulent chief in the fourteenth century.

Opposite Keppoch House, on the north side of the railway,
rises an eminence of 800 feet called Mullroy (in Gaelic:
Maol Ruadh), the hill on which the last clan-battle was
fought in Scotland. The feud was between the MacDonalds
and the MacIntoshes, and this fight was in 1689. The Mac-
Donells of Keppoch were in possession of Glen Roy and
Glen Spean; but the MacIntoshes had from the Crown a

HIGHLAND SHIELING.

written grant of the lands in days gone by. MacIntosh of Moy resolved to assert his rights, and demanded of the rival chief, Coll of Keppoch, by what charter he held the district. MacDonell replied that "he held his lands, not by a sheep's skin, but by the sword." MacIntosh raised his clan, obtained the assistance of a company of independent soldiers enlisted for Government service, and marched into the disputed country. He found Keppoch House deserted, and proceeded to build a fort on the banks of the Roy. His labours were interrupted by the news that the MacDonells, with their kindred, the MacDonalds of Glengarry and of Glencoe, were lying in a narrow glen behind Mullroy, intending to attack the MacIntoshes at dawn. MacIntosh of Moy accordingly led his men up the hill in the dark, but when they had almost surmounted the height, and the grey morning began to show in the sky, they found that the MacDonalds had been up still earlier, and held the upper ridge. As the pipe-tune commemorating the battle puts it, "MacDonald took the brae on them." A fierce fight at once set in, which has thus been described by one of those who fought in the independent company of soldiers on the side of the MacIntosh—a lad who had been with a tobacco-spinner in Inverness, and had run away to enlist. "The MacDonalds came down the hill upon us, without either shoe, stocking, or bonnet on their heads; they gave a shout, and then the fire began on both sides, and continued a hot dispute for an hour (which made me wish I had been spinning tobacco). Then they broke in upon us with sword and target, and Lochaber-axes, which obliged us to give way. Seeing my captain· severely wounded, and a great many men· lying with heads cloven on every side, and having never witnessed the like before, I was sadly affrighted. At length a Highlandman attacked me with sword and target, and cut my wooden-handled bayonet out of the muzzle of my gun. I then clubbed my gun, and gave him a stroke with it, which made the butt end to fly off, and seeing the Highlandmen come fast down upon me, I took to my heels and ran thirty miles before I looked behind me, taking every person whom I saw or met, for my enemy." Commenting on this ingenuous piece of war correspondence, Sir Walter Scott remarks :—" Many, better used to such scenes, fled as far and as fast as Donald MacBane, the tobacco-spinners' apprentice. The gentleman who bore MacIntosh's standard, being a special object of pursuit, saved himself and the sacred deposit by a wonderful exertion; at a place where the River Roy flows between two precipitous rocks, which approach each other over the torrent, he hazarded a desperate leap where no enemy dared follow him, and bore· off his charge in safety. It is said by tradition, that the MacIntoshes fought with much bravery, and that the contest was decided by the desperation of a half-crazed man, called the 'red-haired Bo-man,' or cowherd, whom Keppoch had not summoned to the fight, but who came thither, uncalled, with a club on his shoulder. This man, being wounded by a shot, was so much incensed with the pain, that he darted forward into the thickest of the MacIntoshes, calling out, 'They fly, they fly! Upon them! upon them!' The boldness he displayed, and the strokes he dealt with his unusual weapon, caused the first impression on the array of the enemies of his chief."

The famous Parallel Roads of Glen Roy are reached from here. Keppoch is passed on the left. The residence of its ancient Kings was an island on the Spean. But the river has now changed its course. The garden famous for its pears was destroyed by Cumberland after the '45. Here Viscount Dundee held a council of the Jacobite Chiefs in 1689, and marched at the head of a large .band of warriors to gain a brilliant victory for King James at Killiecrankie, where a silver bullet was said to have ended the mortal career of " Bonnie Dundee."

"Inch" was the home of Colonel Archibald Macdonell, of the 92nd Highlanders, who served with that distinguished corps through the Peninsular War. Two cairns which we passed under St Cyril's, were raised to commemorate his son Ewen, who signalised himself during the Indian Mutiny, and his grandson Alister.

"Tirindrish," on the right, gave its name to the gallant and intrepid Major Donald Macdonald of the '45. He had the honour of firing the first shot for Prince Charlie in the rising of that year. On the 19th August, Major Macdonald, at Highbridge, lower down on the Spean, with a small party of men attacked and took prisoner Captain Scott, of the 1st Regiment of Foot, on his way with a detachment from Fort Augustus to strengthen the garrison at Fort William. Captain Scott was severely wounded, and Major Macdonald sent to the Governor of Fort William for medical aid, which was refused. The generous captor then had his prisoner conveyed to Tirindrish, where every care was bestowed on him, and he was after recovery released on parole, which he faithfully observed. Captain (afterwards General) Scott left an immense fortune to his daughters, the Duchess of Portland and Lady Canning. . In after years he met Major Macdonald's daughter at a Bath assembly, and feelingly described to her how he owed his life to her father's magnanimity, a striking contrast to the conduct of Cumberland's officers and men. Tirindrish was taken prisoner after the battle of Falkirk, with Sir Archibald Primrose, Kinloch, and others, sent to Carlisle, there barbarously despatched, and his head placed on the Scottish Gate, where it remained for many years. His speech on the scaffold, and farewell letters to his friends, give a fine impression of the nobility of his character. In later years Tirindrish was the residence of the Generals Ross

At " Achandaul" lived another Peninsular veteran, Colonel

Mitchell, of the 92nd, who took command of the regiment at Quartre Bras, when Colonel Cameron fell on the 16th June, 1815. He was wounded on that day, and at Waterloo the command of the "gallant Gordons" devolved on Major Macdonald of Dalchosnie, who had the honour of leading them in the celebrated charge, at three o'clock, to face tremendous odds, which is said to have elicited from Napoleon the exclamation, "Les braves Ecossais." The later incident in this charge, the onslaught of the "Scots Greys," is immortalised in Lady Butler's well-known picture, "Scotland for ever." These words were uttered by each of these gallant corps as they passed each other, and in memory of that moment they have ever since dubbed themselves "cousins." Major Macdonald figures in James Grant's "Romance of War."

After passing Keppoch House and Mullroy, a number of

RESTING-CAIRNS, ROY BRIDGE.

little cairns are seen on a heath to the right. These are "resting-cairns"—memorials of the dead—and the importance of the deceased may be gauged by their size. The coffin is carried to the grave in these districts by the relatives and friends, and as the burying-ground is frequently a long way off, the body has to be set down at intervals in order that the bearers may rest. Whenever one of these pauses takes place, each of the mourners gathers a stone, and these stones are all piled up in a "resting-cairn." By counting the stones in one of the heaps the extent of the funeral procession could, therefore, be accurately arrived at. Near these cairns, the line passes through Inver-roy, a picturesque specimen of an old Highland clachan, unspoiled by modern improvements, the white shielings—low thatched huts—scattered at all angles, with the blue peat smoke pouring from their wooden chimneys, while bare-footed and bare-headed bairns toddle about on the brae-side, shouting to each other in Gaelic. The line next crosses the Spean on a three-span bridge. It will interest the traveller who looks down from this bridge on the rapid Spean in summer, to know that in time of spate the water rises nearly twenty feet—to within a few feet of the girders.

The railway now follows the south bank of the Spean until Spean Bridge station is reached (three miles from Roy Bridge), where the river strikes off to the north-west to join the River Lochy, the combined waters flowing south-west and entering Loch Linnhe at Fort William.

At Spean Bridge there is a good hotel, with coach communication to Fort Augustus, the bridge being in the midst of a large pastoral district, while it is also within easy distance of the Caledonian Canal. We are now only some nine miles from Fort William, and are in the very midst of the Lochaber mountains, which are ranged to the south in stupendous groups: Ben Nevis surmounting all, although several of its neighbours are over 4,000 feet in height. All along the glen, from Inverlair, we have been following the course of the romantic Spean, while to the south the vast congregation of mountains has been gradually opening out, glowing in all the colours of the rainbow according to the variations of light and shade; for, bare as a Highland Ben may seem at first sight, it is marvellously tinted, and its many hues melt and change, like the plumage of the "burnished dove," with every new level of the sun's rays and every new change of atmosphere. From Spean Bridge we draw nearer and nearer to Ben Nevis and his brethren, but we lose the river, which disappears to the right down a birch and oak-clad glen. A short distance along this glen lies High Bridge, one of General Wade's famous viaducts, built when he made one of his military roads from Fort

FALLS ON THE SPEAN,
ROY BRIDGE.

William. It was here that the Jacobites, in the '45, had their first skirmish with King George's troops, a party of soldiers marching from Fort Augustus to Fort William having been surprised here by a large body of the Clan Cameron on their way to Glenfinnan, on the west of Loch Eil, where Prince Charlie had that day raised his standard.

The railway now follows, on the right, the public road that stretches from Fort William to Kingussie, and on the left lies General Wade's military road. Presently Inverlochy Castle, the seat of Lord Abinger, is seen on the right, and at this point a magnificent view is obtained—Loch Linnhe, Loch Eil and the Glenfinnan hills in front and Ben Nevis to the left. Presently the famous Nevis distillery is passed, a building no more picturesque than other distilleries, but which inherits a little romance from the fact that it lies in the shadow of the mighty Ben. It stands on the banks of the 'Lochy, that river, swelled by the Spean, descending

THE OLD "LONG JOHN" DISTILLERY.

133

to Loch Linnhe from Loch Lochy. Amongst those who drink that well-known brand of whisky, "Long John," it is often a source of wonder what the name means, so we give tourists the explanation to carry back to the south. Originally the distillery was a smaller establishment, at Millburn, a few miles off, drawing its water from 1,500 feet up the side of the Ben, and its whisky was named "Dew of Ben Nevis." Subsequently the present distillery was built (although the old place is still in existence and in full working) drawing its water from Glen Nevis. The distiller was anxious to get a distinctive name for the new whisky, and he hit upon the title "Long John," as that was the nickname of his grandfather, the original distiller, who was a man six feet four in height.

Just beyond, where the River Lochy pours its waters into Loch Linnhe, stands an old ruin on the bank—the original Inverlochy Castle, a seat of the "Black Comyns" until they were driven out by Robert the Bruce. According to Mrs. MacKellar, "Tradition says that it was built in one night by the Picts, and that their Kings resided there; that King Achaius, who was a contemporary of Charlemagne, signed a treaty there with that monarch, which is still seen among the archives of Paris; and that sixteen gentlemen of the name of Comyn witnessed the treaty." The ruin we now see was certainly not built by the Picts, either in one night or at leisure; we should fix its date in the thirteenth century. Little beyond the four bare walls are now left, with towers at the corners about thirty feet high. The western is known as "Comyn's Tower," and has walls ten feet thick, while the internal diameter is eight paces, but this tower is larger than the rest. The old keep is picturesquely situated at the water's edge, and must

THE RIVER LOCHY.

have been a place of great importance in the old days. It was near here that James I. of Scotland, in 1429, defeated Alexander, the Lord of the Isles, and Earl of Ross, who had invaded Lochaber with ten thousand men. Two years after, the Islesmen returned under Donald Balloch, again invaded Lochaber, and at Inverlochy utterly defeated the Earls of Mar

OLD INVERLOCHY CASTLE AND BEN NEVIS.

and Caithness, although numbers were in favour of the Royal leaders. Donald Dhu or Black Donald, the Chief of Lochiel, fought on the defeated side, and readers will remember Scott's "Pibroch of Donald Dhu," words written for a very ancient pibroch of the Camerons, calling the clan to battle:—

"Leave untended the herd,
  The flock without shelter;
Leave the corpse uninterr'd,
  The bride at the altar;
Leave the deer, leave the steer,
  Leave nets and barges:
Come with your fighting gear,
  Broadswords and targes.

"Come from the deep glen, and
  From mountain so rocky,
The war-pipe and pennon
  Are at Inverlochy.
Come every hill-plaid, and
  True heart that wears one,
Come every steel blade, and
  Strong hand that bears one."

But the most famous fight at Inverlochy was fought in February, 1645, in the time of the Covenanters, between the Marquis of Montrose—"the Great Marquis "—on the Royalist side, and the Duke of Argyll for the Covenant. When winter came on, the Duke of Argyll sent his army into winter quarters and retired to his own castle of Inverary, in fancied security, thinking idly that Montrose could do nothing until spring; but the Marquis, with an army of Highlanders, "wading through drifts of snow, scaling precipices, and traversing the mountain paths, known to none save the solitary shepherd or huntsman," forced an entry into Argyllshire, which he laid waste with fire and sword, causing even Argyll himself to flee in a fishing-boat. "Montrose," writes Sir Walter Scott, "continued the work of revenge for nearly a month, and, then concluding he had destroyed the influence which Argyll, by the extent of his power, and the supposed strength of his country, possessed over the minds of the Highlanders, withdrew towards Inverness, with the purpose of organizing a general gathering of the clans. But he had scarce made this movement, when he learned that his rival, Argyll, had returned into the Western Highlands with some Lowland forces ; that he had called around him his numerous clan, burning to revenge the wrongs which they had sustained, and was lying with a strong force near the old castle of Inverlochy, situated at the western extremity of the chain of lakes, through which the Caledonian Canal is now conducted. The news at once altered Montrose's plans. He returned upon Argyll by a succession of the most difficult mountain passes covered with snow ; and the vanguard of the Campbells saw themselves suddenly engaged with that of their implacable enemy. Both parties lay all night on their arms ; but, by break of day, Argyll betook himself to his galley, and rowing off shore, remained a spectator of the combat when, by all the rules of duty and gratitude, he ought to have been at the head of his devoted followers. His unfortunate clansmen supported the honour of the name with the greatest courage, and many of the most distinguished fell on the field of battle Montrose gained a complete victory, which greatly extended his influence over the Highlands, and in proportion diminished that of his discomfited rival." The story of the battle will be found in the "Legend of Montrose," told with full detail and enlivened by graphic incident; our present quotation is from the "Tales of a Grandfather." There is a curious link between this battle of Inverlochy and the Keppoch murder, the tale of which we related before. The man who guided the army of Montrose through those snow-blocked passes, hitherto regarded as impenetrable, was Ian Lom, the Keppoch bard, who wreaked such summary vengeance on the seven murderers. It is he who is supposed to be the speaker in Professor Aytoun's famous ballad, "The Execution of Montrose:"—

> " Come hither, Evan Cameron!
>   Come stand beside my knee—
> I hear the river roaring down
>   Towards the wintry sea
> There's shouting on the mountain-side
>   There's war within the blast—
> Old faces look upon me,
>   Old forms go trooping past :
> I hear the pibroch wailing
>   Amidst the din of fight,
> And my dim spirit wakes again
>   Upon the verge of night.

> " 'Twas I that led the Highland host
>   Through wild Lochaber's snows,
> What time the plaided-clans came down
>   To battle with Montrose
> I've told thee how the Southrons fell
>   Beneath the broad claymore,
> And how we smote the Campbell clan
>   By Inverlochy's shore.
> I've told thee how we swept Dundee,
>   And tamed the Lindsay's pride;
> But never have I told thee yet
>   How the great Marquis died."

These warlike stanzas do not agree, however, with the tradition as to Ian's attitude at the battle. Having guided Montrose through the passes, he felt that his mission was ended. His Chief bade him take a claymore and join in the assault; but he declined, on the ground that if he were killed there would be nobody to sing the victory. It is satisfactory to know that he duly composed a wild Gaelic pæan when the battle was won, and thus justified his theory that the pen was mightier·than the sword.

In 1431, these battlements saw another well-fought field, for here the Royal forces under Alexander, Earl of Mar, were defeated by the Lord of the Isles This family, then at the summit of its power, aimed at nothing less than the sovereignty of Scotland. The pipe tune, "Piproch Dhonuill Duibh," translated by Scott, was composed for the victor on this occasion. The Castle is supposed to date from the thirteenth century, but the site was long a Royal fortress of very great antiquity In early ages much communication was carried on between this and France and Spain. Treaties with Charlemagne are said to have been signed here by some of the ancient Scottish Kings. On the opposite side of the River Lochy we can see the long stretch of moor, and here was once the loch which gave the district its name—a name evidently of great antiquity, as "Adamnan" in his life of St. Columba, of whom he was the seventh successor, mentions the Saint's journey to the "Aberach Land" This work lay undiscovered for a thousand years in a monastery on the Lake of Constance.

The hills of Loch Arkaig and of Achnacarry are seen to the right, the country of the Clan Cameron. By Sir Allan Cameron of Erracht, a cadet of Lochiel, the 79th Cameron Highlanders were raised in the end of the last century. Their achievements have many times been written on the roll of fame, since Byron wrote on Waterloo, "when wild and high the Camerons' gathering rose." The tartan is a beautiful blend of the two clans of the district, Cameron and Macdonald. The Cameron men were once so numerous as to almost justify the strange reply given to a belated but suspected traveller who in a wild night of storm and sleet besought·entrance to a solitary house. "Are there no Christians here?" he demanded piteously. "No, no," was the stern answer, "we are all Camerons here."

After passing Inverlochy we enter Fort William—a hundred miles from the start—the railway passing through the old fort, now dismantled, from which the place takes its name. The town is a minute one, with a population of only about 2,000, but it looks quite an imposing city after the wilderness we have come through. The houses straggle along the shore of Loch Linnhe, the wide arm of the sea that stretches up from Mull; but the township is well supplied with hotels; and, as Aunt Gilchrist says in William Black's "In Far Lochaber" —"It's a grand place for being in the middle of things." Now that the West Highland Railway has been constructed, it will be more in the middle of things than ever. The railway, after passing through the fort, runs along an esplanade to the pier, thus making connection with MacBrayne's fine service of steamers, by which the traveller may go south to Oban, and round through the Kyles of Bute to Craigendoran, whence he started on the West Highland Railway; or will take him north by the beautiful route of the Caledonian Canal to Inverness. For those who come to Fort William by steamer, from either north or south, there is the West Highland to take them east through Lochaber, and

A GLIMPSE OF FORT WILLIAM.

south by the route we have traversed, with all its possibilities in the way of diversions to right or left. Apart altogether from its proximity to such notable scenes as Glencoe, Glen Nevis, Glen Finnan, Glen Spean, Glen Roy and Achnacarry, and the fact that it lies at the very base of Ben Nevis, Fort William is certainly "in the middle of things."

The little township has sprung up around the fort, which was originally built by General Monck, in Cromwell's time, as a rude fortification of turf, to act as a base for the troops sent to keep in subjection Evan Dhu of Lochiel, the Chief of the Camerons, who stood out like a Scottish Hereward against the forces of the Commonwealth, long after the other clans had submitted. Many a fierce skirmish between Lochiel and the Sassenach red-coats took place around Fort William and Inverlochy, the Highlanders generally getting the best of it, as is recorded in Scott's "Tales of a Grandfather." In the time of William the Third the fort was rebuilt in its present form (or rather its late form, for the railway works have cut much of it up) by General Mackay, who was afterwards defeated by Viscount Dundee at Killiecrankie. It was a strong fortification of its kind, with ditch, glacis and ravelin, of which portions may yet be seen, mounting fifteen twelve-pounders and with a regular garrison of about a hundred men: while in times of trouble many more soldiers were thrown into it. Both in the '15 and the '45 it was besieged by the Jacobites, but was never taken. Some interesting particulars of the second siege will be found in Mrs. MacKellar's handbook. "There was no village here," says this authority, "previous to the erection of Cromwell's fort. Then some houses began to arise on the face of the hill. Afterwards, when the present fort was built, the people were encouraged to erect houses there, to form a village to be a sutlery to it. They might build where and how they liked, only the houses were to be composed of turf and wattle, so as to be easily set on fire in case of a rising, or of an enemy effecting a lodgment there. This village was demolished, and then the people began to build at the seaside, where the lower streets of the town are now, and the free charters given them accounts for the irregularity of the buildings, which, from the sea, look so disorderly." Various attempts have been made to re-name the town after it was raised to the dignity of a burgh of barony. First it was called Maryburgh, in honour of William's Consort; but it remained Fort William, in honour of William himself. Later, the Duke of Gordon was made superior of the township, and it was called Gordonsburgh; but it remained Fort William. Afterwards Sir Duncan Cameron became superior, and called it Duncansburgh; but it still remained Fort William. We do not think there is any reason to regret the popular rejection of the three names suggested.

Fort William lies too close to Ben Nevis for a good view

MARMORE DEER FOREST, FROM GLEN NEVIS.

of that mountain to be obtained, but the scenery is magnificent without that crowning attraction. William Black has thus sketched the view as it first presented itself to the heroine of " In Far Lochaber " :—" When they took her along to 'the Craigs,' and ascended the mound there, she was struck dumb by the singular and varied and luminous beauty of the vast panorama extending away in every direction. The wild hills of Lochaber were all aflame in the sunset light; dark amid trees stood the ruins of Inverlochy Castle; the shallow waters before her stretched away up to Corpach, where a flood of golden radiance came pouring out of Loch Eil; while all along the west, and as far south as Ardgour, the mountains were deepening and deepening in shadow, making the glow in the sky overhead all the more dazzlingly brilliant . . . . Might there not be in heaven, high hills like these, flame-smitten with rose and gold, and placid lakes reflecting their awful and silent splendour? . . . . Those roseate summits seemed so far away; they were hardly of this earth; they were God's footstool, removed beyond the habitations and the knowledge of men." In that book of William Black's, much about Fort William and the surrounding neighbourhood will be found, told in that flowing and enthusiastic style of his, which conveys such vivid impressions of scenery, although it cannot be compared with the wonderful word-painting of Blackmore in his descriptions of Dartmoor.

As seen from the Fort William side, Ben Nevis appears a somewhat shapeless mountain, piled shoulder on shoulder, in vast folds of granite into the sky, as if disdaining symmetrical form, and depending on sheer bulk alone to vindicate its grandeur. It is only when it is observed how seldom the summit can be seen free of clouds, that the gigantic height of the Ben is realised (4,406 feet), for it is the highest mountain in the United Kingdom; and it is only when a pedestrian attempts to walk round it, and finds that the base is more than twenty-four miles in circumference, that its colossal bulk is fully grasped. For three-fourths of the ascent the mountain is of red granite, the remaining fourth being of porphyry, "which weathers of a brown colour, but when newly fractured shows bluish and greenish tints, mottled with specks of white felspar." The ascent may be made either from Fort William or from Banavie, about three miles distant, to which there is a branch line of the West Highland Railway, but the feat should not be attempted without a guide, as the densest of mists descend on the mountain without a minute's warning, and render the position of the mountain climber extremely dangerous. It is proposed to build a railway to the summit, similar to that which ascends the Rigi; but it has not yet got beyond the stage of contemplation.

To reach the summit of Ben Nevis means a climb of five miles up a bridle path, on so steep a gradient that in the distance named there is a rise of over 4,000 feet. This is not a task for a weak-lunged or weak-legged man; but the

BEN CRUACHAN.

142

journey may be partly done on a hill-pony, and at the top there is a small Temperance Hotel, with sleeping accommodation for over a dozen guests, where tea, bed, and breakfast may be obtained for half-a-guinea—a small sum to pay for the proud boast in future years that you have slept on the top of Ben Nevis! The view from the summit is a bewildering one, for the eye looks down on nothing but mountain peaks, except where they are broken by the three great sheets of water—Loch Linnhe, Loch Eil and Loch Lochy, or by the sea itself. To take up again a former simile, it is like standing in the "ball" of St. Paul's, and gazing on the endless miles of the roofs of London, for the hill tops below seem interminable, and might almost be called

LOOKING TOWARDS THE HEAD OF GLEN NEVIS.

monotonous in their multitude. On a clear day the eye can trace in the north-east the form of Ben MacDhui, the second mountain in Britain, which rises to a height of 4,296 feet in the Braemar Highlands. To the north the vision ranges as far as Ben Wyvis in Ross-shire. Westward, the Cuillin Hills in Skye may be distinguished, and in particularly favourable weather, some of the heights in the Outer Hebrides, ninety miles away. Southward may be distinguished Ben Cruachan, at the head of Loch Awe, lying almost east of Oban. Southwest may be seen the Islands, and even a glimpse of Ireland may be caught. It is a prospect astounding in its wide expanse, and he is lucky who reaches the summit of Ben Nevis on a day when the atmosphere permits of a good view. Frequently the hill-top is shrouded in dense mist, giving on the wall of fog an effect as of the well-known Spectre of the Brocken. On the Ben itself there is a magnificent chasm to be inspected—a perpendicular precipice, ranging from 1,500 to 2,000 feet in depth, which Sir Robert Christison has described as the finest precipice in the world.

On the summit of Ben Nevis is the Observatory, where two meteorologists keep watch on the weather day and night, summer and winter, watch and watch about, so that hourly readings of the instruments may be taken, and telegraphed

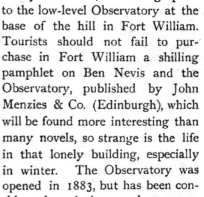

to the low-level Observatory at the base of the hill in Fort William. Tourists should not fail to purchase in Fort William a shilling pamphlet on Ben Nevis and the Observatory, published by John Menzies & Co. (Edinburgh), which will be found more interesting than many novels, so strange is the life in that lonely building, especially in winter. The Observatory was opened in 1883, but has been considerably enlarged since, and now presents the appearance of a primitive fort, surmounted at one end by a watch tower thirty feet high. It is provisioned for nine months, as it is frequently cut off for many weeks at a time from all communication with the world below, while even in the middle of summer the transport of stores is no easy task. As

OLD FIR TREES
IN GLEN NEVIS.

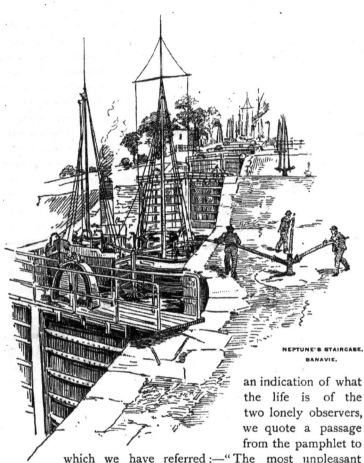

NEPTUNE'S STAIRCASE,
BANAVIE.

an indication of what the life is of the two lonely observers, we quote a passage from the pamphlet to which we have referred :—" The most unpleasant weather is when it rains while the temperature is still below freezing. The rain then freezes as it falls, and everything gets covered with hard ice, which may increase in thickness indefinitely, the only limit being the time that these conditions continue. On one occasion it lasted for two days, and the ice was more than a foot thick, both on the ground and on the windward side of all projections. . . . . During the months of February and March it is not uncommon to have south-easterly gales blowing for three or four days continuously, at the rate of eighty to a hundred miles an hour; but under these circumstances the hill-top is usually swept at once clear of all loose snow, and a hard surface of rough ice left, on which good footing may be got. At first, when the surface was icy, and the wind very strong, the observers used to go out roped together, but experience has shown that even in the most violent gusts, safety may be got by lying down. . . . . On the night of the 21st of February, 1885, a terrific southerly gale blew with hurricane force, and stopped all outside observation for fifteen hours. It was impossible to stand or even to crawl to windward, while the most carefully shielded lantern was blown out at once. During the height of the gale the air was full of snowdrift, intermixed with which were great lumps of hardened snow that had been torn from the ground by the violence of the wind. One of these flying pieces broke the only window that was above the snow."

It is from Banavie (pronounced with the accent on the first syllable), about three miles north-east of Fort William, lying on the Caledonian Canal, that the best view of Ben Nevis may be obtained, and to Banavie there is, as we have said, a short branch line of the West Highland Railway. The position of Banavie at the junction of Loch Eil and Loch Linnhe—giving magnificent views each way—and its uniformly bright aspect, forces the impression that among the earliest developments which the railway communication will ensure, will be the growing importance of this favourably placed village as a tourist centre for the Mid-Western Highlands.

Leaving Fort William, the line crosses the Lochy at old Inverlochy Castle, and traverses the bare Corpach Moss, to the side of the Canal, where the famous " Neptune's Staircase " is to be seen, the grand finale of the artificial water-way. It consists of eight locks, end to end, each with a drop of eight feet of water, so that a vessel entering the chain changes its level sixty-four feet before it resumes sailing in the open. The delay is, of course, considerable : but the tourist has no reason to grumble, for he finds close by " Neptune's Stair-case " an exceedingly comfortable hotel—the " Lochiel Arms," which has bedroom accommodation for over a hundred guests. From the windows he has the fine view of Ben Nevis, of which we have spoken. From this point of view the form of the mountain is majestic in the extreme, and its contour may be traced from the radiant heather-clad base to the snow-capped summit lost in the clouds. An amusing anecdote is told by Mrs. MacKellar, who writes, "It is said that the ancient charter, by which the proprietor of the mountain held his land, gave him it as long as there was snow on Ben Nevis, and that one year so little snow had fallen in winter, and the summer was so hot, that he had to put a tent over a snow-wreath to keep it from melting, lest his tenure of the land would be gone." It is seldom such a precaution is necessary!

As a souvenir of Banavie, we may give the tourist the explanation of why a lobster is known in the West Highlands as a "Banavie Flea." A good many years ago an American was stopping in the Banavie hotel, and he made himself very obnoxious by his contemptuous remarks on Scottish scenery. "Ben Nevis?" he said; "do you call that a mountain? You should see our mighty Rockies! Loch Linnhe? do you call that a lake? You should see our Lake Superior! Rannoch Moor? do you call that a plain? You should see our western prairies!" and so he went on, to the intense exasperation of the Highland waiter, who went and procured a live lobster (for they are caught occa-

A BANAVIE FLEA.

sionally in the Loch) which he secreted, in requital of the insults, in the American's bed. Hardly had the American gone to sleep when the lobster caught him by the toe with a grasp like a vice. He jumped out of bed with a yell and rang for the boots. "Boots," he said solemnly, rubbing his toe as he spoke, "you may not have such big mountains and big lakes and big plains here as we have in the States, but you have the most tarnation big fleas I ever experienced."

From Fort William there are various attractive day trips, one of the most notable being up Glen Nevis, along which a coach runs for about six miles. The Glen is a very wild and picturesque one, threaded by the crystal waters of the River Nevis, and used to be a favourite pasture for goats, which found in the precipices a congenial home. At Achariach, about six miles up, beyond the Druidical "rocking-stone" and the ancient vitrified fort, are the Lower Falls of Nevis, a beautiful cascade, and a mile further on is one of the most striking waterfalls in the Kingdom, a stream foaming down the side of Ben Nevis at an angle of about sixty degrees, for a distance of about 1,000 feet. After passing a cave, about which there is some very curious folk-lore, a rough walk of about two miles brings the traveller to the Upper Falls of Nevis, which have a stupendous drop of about 500 feet, not unlike that of the Falls of Foyers. Another enjoyable trip is up Glenfinnan, seventeen miles, to the spot where Prince Charlie raised his standard in the '45 ; going along Loch Eil to Glenfinnan, passing by the old house—Fassifern—long the residence of Sir Ewan Cameron, the gallant soldier who was killed while commanding his regiment at Quatre Bras. A monument now marks the spot—"more like an old lighthouse than anything else," as the writer of Baddeley's Guide aptly says, crowned by a figure of the Prince himself, looking up the Glen for the Camerons, who had been delayed by the skirmish at Highbridge we mentioned before. At Fassifern Prince Charlie spent a night of his weary wanderings on his way to the safe shelter on Ben Alder. From the ramparts too, we can see across the Loch near Banavie, a spot which preserves the memory of Shakespeare's murdered Banquo, Thane of Lochaber. It is called "Banquo's walk." His son Fleance fled to Brittany, whence his descen- ' dants returned in the train of William the Conqueror, and later to their native land as the Stuart Kings of Scotland. Lochaber is thus the cradle of our Royal race. Yet another tempting drive is, twelve and a half miles to the "Dark Mile of Achnacarry," a magnificent avenue of trees, like a cathedral aisle, the branches joining and forming an umbrageous roof. But to sketch the attractions that lie around Fort William would be an endless task. In whatever direction the traveller sets out he will be thoroughly satisfied with the day's experience when he returns to his hotel at night.

INVERLOCHY CASTLE—OLD AND NEW.

A Trip Thro' Glencoe

"When the herd of frantic women
  Stumbled through the midnight snow,
With their father's houses blazing,
  And their dearest dead below !
Oh, the horror of the tempest,
  As the flashing drift was blown,
Crimsoned with the conflagration,
  And the roofs went thundering down !"

AYTOUN—"The Widow of Glencoe."

FEW names appeal more vividly to the imagination than that of Glencoe—the scene of the infamous massacre in the days of William and Mary. The fascination of the name is greatly due to the historical associations that linger round the place, but only partly so, for the scenery of the Glen is universally admitted to be amongst the most impressive in these grand and solemn Western Highlands. Although the memory of the massacre undoubtedly deepens the feeling of awe with which the traveller views the terrible beauties of the Glen, yet the pass will never be forgotten by those who traverse it, quite apart from the sombre recollections that cling to it. So striking are its features that it stands apart from all other Highland glens, unapproachable in lonely majesty; and even to a stranger, ignorant of the story of the massacre, its gloomy depths are filled with the spirit of tragedy. Macaulay, in a brilliant passage, has painted the aspect of the Glen as it presents itself to the imaginative visitor who realises to the full the fitness of the spot for the scene of an historical crime. "In the Gaelic tongue, Glencoe signifies the Glen of Weeping; and in truth that pass is the most dreary and melancholy of all the Scottish passes—the very Valley of the Shadow of Death. Mists and storms brood over it through the greater part of the finest summer; and even

on those rare days when the sun is bright, and when there
is no cloud in the sky, the impression made by the landscape is sad and awful. The path lies along a stream which
issues from the most sullen and gloomy of mountain pools.
Huge precipices of naked stone frown on both sides. Even
in July the streaks of snow may often be discerned in the

BEN NEVIS FROM LOCH LINNHE.

rifts near the summits. All down the sides of the crags heaps
of ruin mark the headlong paths of the torrents. Mile after
mile the only sound that indicates life is the faint cry of a
bird of prey from some storm-beaten pinnacle of rock. The
progress of civilisation, which has turned so many wastes
into fields yellow with harvests, or gay with apple blossoms,
has only made Glencoe more desolate."

At Fort William the tourist is almost on the threshold
of the Glen. A steamer will take him down Loch Linnhe

BRIDGE OF ORCHY.

some ten miles to
Ballachulish, and
there he will find a
coach service running
through to Bridge of
Orchy, where the
railway may again
be entered upon.
Until the railway
made a through route
possible, the coaches
from Ballachulish

used to run only to the mouth of the Glen, and then returned, tourists never seeing its real magnificence — a fact that accounts for the feeling of comparative disappointment that some travellers have expressed. Now a drive is offered that has no rival in the kingdom for grandeur and variety of prospect, and no one should miss it.

At the pier of Ballachulish the coach meets the steamer; but before mounting, the tourist should see the spot of the "Appin Murder" already referred to, where Colin Campbell of Glenure, collecting rents on confiscated estates, was shot. The coach travels along the shores of Loch Leven, affording a wonderful view of the mountains of Ardgour and Appin, and in about a mile Ballachulish hotel is reached, where the tourist has an opportunity of fortifying himself against the long journey before him. Near the Loch Leven Hotel,

ENTRANCE TO LOCH LEVEN, ARGYLLSHIRE.

on the other side of the ferry, stands a knoll where James Stewart of the Glens was hanged for the Appin Murder, although he appears to have had nothing to do with it. Presently the famous slate quarries are passed, and the road strikes inland to where rises the "Pap of Glencoe," marking the commencement of the Glen. The valley, in its earlier stretches, is a placid example of Highland scenery, quite distinct from the dark and stupendous gorge that is coming. Soon the River Coe, or Cona, is met, and is followed the remainder of the way as it threads the Glen, as a swift and narrow stream rushing to Loch Leven from the mountains of the pass. At Invercoe Bridge, between four and five miles from Ballachulish, the Glen is entered, and the scene of the massacre is reached. Around the bridge lies the little village of Carnach, which was the chief clachan of the Macdonalds of Glencoe, a scattered collection of stone huts, mostly with whitewashed walls, the brown thatch weighted with stones to prevent its being blown clean away by the storms that come roaring down the Glen, uprooting tall fir trees in their course. To this day the inhabitants of these quaint little cottages are Macdonalds almost to a man, but the quiet and picturesque village is no longer a hot-bed of

THE BUCHAILLE ETIVE, GLENCOE.

Highland turbulence. Yet, when the massacre took place, it presented an appearance almost equally peaceful, for no mischief was intended by the chief, and no danger was suspected.

The gruesome story of the massacre is familiar, but its circumstances will bear recapitulation in aid of the visitor's memory. When William of Orange was attempting the pacification of the Jacobite Highlands, he offered an indemnity to all the Highland chiefs who submitted and took the oath of allegiance before the last day of December 1691 ; threatening

destruction by fire and sword to those who remained mal-
content. One by one the chiefs submitted and subscribed to
the oath, but MacIan, the aged chief of the Glencoe branch
of the Macdonalds, obstinately held out until the last moment.
But on the 31st of December he realised the folly of resisting
longer, seeing that he now stood alone, and he presented
himself at Fort William to take the oath. But there was no
magistrate in the garrison, and his appearance on the last
day of grace was therefore useless, according to the letter
of the proclamation. Grasping the danger of the position in
which he had placed himself, MacIan set out at once for
Inverary, where the nearest magistrate was to be found, but
it was a long and rough journey for the old man in mid-
winter, through mountain passes deep with snow, and he did
not reach there until the 6th of January. After some hesita-
tion by the magistrate, he was allowed to take the oath, and
the certificate of his submission was forwarded to Edinburgh,
accompanied by full explanation of the circumstances. But
MacIan and his men had made too many enemies by their
depredations. The certificate was pronounced null and void
by the authorities, and a body of troops was despatched
to Glencoe, with secret orders to "extirpate that set of
thieves." MacIan, happy in the knowledge that he had
taken the oath, suspected no evil when 120 men were
quartered on his clachan, the more so as the commander was
Captain Campbell, of Glenlyon, uncle to his son's wife: and
for nearly a fortnight he entertained the band with Highland
hospitality. On the very night of the massacre, Captain
Campbell sat up playing cards with the chief's sons, so
friendly was the intercourse between the soldiers and the
clansmen. Meanwhile, arrangements were being made at Fort
William for closing the lines of retreat from Glencoe, and
at five o'clock on the morning of the 13th February the signal
for massacre was given. In cold blood the soldiers dragged
their hosts from bed and slaughtered them, between thirty
and forty perishing, including a number of women. From the
aged chief to a boy of twelve, all who could be secured were
slain, while the women, young children, and a few old men,
over seventy years of age, were driven into the mountains to

perish of cold and hunger. It is one of the most brutal deeds recorded in the history of even the most barbaric times, and the horror of the story seems to grow still greater when one stands on the scene, wrapped in the silence of the Glen. Near the bridge rises a knoll covered with huts, and on the summit, overlooking the swift waters of the Cona, stands an Ionic cross of red granite, raised in 1883, in memory of the victims, by a direct descendant of the murdered chief. Scattered over the Glen may yet be seen the blackened

LOCH LEVEN AND THE PAP OF GLENCOE.

ruins of the huts in which the Macdonalds were massacred, dumb witnesses to the horrors of that winter morning.

Immediately around the village of Carnach the hills, covered with moss and heather, are comparatively gentle in contour, while in parts the valley is wooded; but looking up the Glen a very different aspect is seen. Great jutting peaks of black rock rise stern and forbidding, frowning against the sky, the gateways of the real Glencoe, casting a gloom over the softer landscape. As we approach these grim portals, grand as the colossal chasms imagined by the weird mind of Gustave Doré in his attempt to realise Dante's "Vision of the Inferno," another glen is seen striking off to the right—Glen Leich-na-moie—up which the fugitives from the massacre fled, pursued by the merciless troops. The road here plunges into the wilderness of the Pass of Glencoe, shut in by dark and terrible crags, rising sheer from the Glen like enormous masses of bronze, on which vegetation can find no root-hold. Down their rugged sides are the grey scars marking the course of mountain torrents, which have piled at the foot of the precipices great heaps of rocky *débris*, black as coal. At the mouth of the Glen is a small but well-appointed and comfortable hotel, which will be found a good stopping place for those who wish to spend a few days in a closer study of the unparalleled scenery of Glencoe, than can be made by the passing coach traveller. This hotel stands on a ridge overlooking both the view to Ballachulish and that towards the Black Mount, and as we descend the declivity, into the depths of the pass, it is like saying good-bye to the sun. By the side of the road runs the Cona, blue as an Italian sky, pouring from a tarn called Loch Triochatan, deep sunk in the valley. The extraordinary depth of the blue, in both loch and stream, is due to the dark bed, the black rock being washed down in sand from the hills.

THE LOCH IN GLENCOE.

As we speed through the Glen, its marvellous grandeur grows upon us, and our wonder increases at its completeness as an epitome of all the most impressive features of Highland landscape. On either side rise frightful precipices, gloomy as night. Down the Glen rushes a mountain torrent, while from either side pours another: the three mingling in a foaming turmoil at the same point into the main gorge, the conflux being known as "the Meeting of the Waters." On the north

GLENCOE: "THE CHANCELLOR" AND OSSIAN'S CAVE.

—the right as we ascend the Glen—rise three stern peaks of blackest rock, their giant bulks, separated by steep and narrow corries, placed side by side as barriers to the Glen. These peaks projecting like buttresses into the valley, of which their wide-spread bases form one boundary, are known as the "Three Sisters," or otherwise as "Faith, Hope, and Charity," in grimly ironical tribute to their similarity in severity of outline. The corrie that intervenes between the first and second of the "Sisters," marks the boundary between the two famous deer-forests of Dalness and Black Mount, while the precipitous cleft between the second and third is known as the "Reivers' Glen," as it used to be a favourite retreat amongst the caterans for the concealment of stolen cattle. The discovery of a horse-shoe near the top of the corrie gives evidence of the truth of this story, although it seems an almost impossible path for a horse. High on the rocky face of the first "Sister" is Ossian's Cave, a natural aperture about eight feet deep, which looks from below like an enormous keyhole cut in the black precipice. It owes its name to the tradition that Ossian was born on the banks of the Cona, a stream of which he certainly sang with great enthusiasm. According to the folk-lore of Glencoe, the women in the olden time were wont to perambulate the cave, and spinning, when following the goats. If this be so, the women of that time must have been even more nimble than their flock, for the cave is at a giddy height in the side of a sheer precipice. A man of great daring and experience in climbing can, however, reach it, indeed the old shepherd in the cottage lying in the valley below has been in it in his younger days. Where this shepherd's cottage now stands there used to be a hut, in which the wife of MacIan died, on the day after the massacre, killed partly by grief and partly by violence, for the soldiers had treated her so roughly that they tore her rings from her fingers with their teeth. Turning to the mighty crags on the other side of the Glen, the Appin side, we see a marvellously effective piece of natural portraiture in the peak of a mountain called "The Chancellor." A vast rock on the summit forms the head and shoulders of a burly, strong featured, short bearded man, wearing a judicial wig. From one point of view a speaking likeness of the Marquis of Salisbury is presented, and a little further on, the face elongates into an almost equally good representation of the late Lord Iddesleigh.

As the third "Sister" is passed—the sentinel of the Glen at the eastern end — the road climbs steeply until at the very gateway of the pass a level platform is reached, sur-rounded by a low parapet, standing a considerable height above the bed of the Cona This is known as "The Study," and from it a glorious view of the Glen is seen. It lies at our feet in sublime desolation, stretching westwards mile on mile towards Ballachulish. We do not know where in the confines of the United Kingdom a more savage and impres-sive landscape is to be found. There is a weird solemnity about the scene that baffles description, a spirit of loneliness and sadness, strangely appropriate to the memories of the Glen, and it is with reluctance that we tear ourselves away from the vision of that steep and sombre valley, with its flashing streams and its gleaming tarn, hemmed in by a stern

"FAITH, HOPE & CHARITY."—GLENCOE.

array of rugged pinnacles and crags, their sides scarred by seams and fissures that seem to speak of suffering, like the deep lines of care on the face of a strong man.

On emerging from Glencoe the road winds down hill, through a wild and picturesque country, in the midst of the great hills of the Black Mount. On the left may be seen the remains of a rough track made by General Wade, as an approach over the hills to Fort William. It is known as the "Devil's Staircase," and it was up that way that the two young sons of MacIan fled in escaping from the massacre, when their father was shot in his bed in their house in Glen Leich-na-moie. Barefoot, they ran up the bridle path along Glencoe, climbed the hills at the Devil's Staircase, and did

KINGSHOUSE AND THE BUCHAILLE ETIVE.

not stop until they reached Fersit on Loch Treig. As Kingshouse is approached, attention centres on two commanding mountains on the right, vast angular masses of black rock, crowned by pyramidal summits. These are the two "Etive Herds," or herdsmen. The greater is the famous Buchaille Etive, the Big Herd, and it stands on ward, dominating the surrounding eminences, at the mouth of Glen Etive, which strikes off to Loch Etive. By its side, almost identical in shape, is the "Little Herd," small only by comparison, for both are well over 3,000 feet.

Opposite Buchaille Etive lies the Kingshouse Hotel, a homely and comfortable inn, which is a very pleasant discovery in this forsaken waste. It is called Kingshouse because General Wade stopped there when engaged in his great work of road-making through the wilds; and it will be found an admirable stopping-place for the tourist who wishes to examine at leisure the glories of Glencoe, for it lies only an hour's walk from the "Study." The trout fishing is unusually good, a basket of six dozen in a five-hours' day being a common event.

After a stoppage for refreshments, the coach resumes its course through the moorland desert, skirting on the right the Black Mount Hills, and obtaining on the left a magnificent view of Rannoch Moor, its vast expanse broken in the foreground by a chain of little lochs. About two miles and a

RANNOCH MOOR, FROM THE ROAD THROUGH GLENCOE.

half from Kingshouse a point of the road is reached known in Gaelic as the "Shoulder of the Grey Fir," which is said to be the highest carriage road in the country. Farther on a mountain torrent, called the Corrie Ba, and running from a hill called Stobh Goil, is crossed, and is distinguished as the longest running water in Scotland. It passes through Loch Ba, Loch Lydoch, Loch Rannoch and Loch Tummel, joining the Tay near Ballinluig, and entering the sea at Perth. Of course its original name is soon lost, but its waters run well over a hundred miles before reaching the ocean. About ten miles from Kingshouse, Inveroran is reached, a cheerful little hotel lying at the south-western extremity of Loch Tulla —where good fishing may be obtained. It was about a mile above Inveroran that Duncan Ban MacIntyre, the Gaelic poet, was born, at the beginning of the last century. Three miles beyond Inveroran, the coach comes to Bridge of Orchy, after a run of about thirty miles, and the West Highland Railway takes up the traveller to carry him north or south as he will. These thirty miles of stupendous wilderness, peopled only by deer, the mountain hare, and wild fowl, have formed a fitting finale to the unique journey we have sketched, and of this we are sure, that whoever follows us over the hitherto unbeaten track we have traced, will look back on the experience with lingering memory for many a year to come.

IN GLENCOE.

LIGHTHOUSE AT CORRAN FERRY.

SOME CHARACTERISTICS OF HIGHLAND SCENERY.

An Essay written by the late REV. NORMAN MACLEOD, D.D., *for " Mountain Loch and Glen," the Illustrations of the Scottish Lochs being by* JOSEPH ADAM.

THERE are no places in the world better known to the traveller or more admired than the Highlands and Islands of Scotland. They form a portion of the "grand tour" of those in search of the sublime or the beautiful in nature.

It is almost unnecessary to define, geographically, the

LOCH KATRINE.

"Highlands." When the traveller, on a clear day, gazes northward and westward from the battlements of Edinburgh Castle, he sees the advanced sentinels of the giant army of Highland mountains that lie beyond. When he journeys to Glasgow there suddenly bursts upon his view, immediately after passing Falkirk, a wonderfully beautiful alluvial plain, rich in woods and signs of busy industry, ramparted along the north by the Ochils and the Trossachs Hills, as it were an advanced line of the Grampian range. This is the very junction of the Lowlands and Highlands. When he sails down the Firth of Clyde, he has to the north, opposite Greenock and onwards, the hills of the true Highlands rolling in beautiful outlines across the sky, and at the Kyles of Bute rising abruptly from the shore, penetrated by the oft-repeated Highland Loch in all its glory, he enters at once, through the *dorus mohr*, or great door, the Western Highlands proper, with scattered islands, racing tideways, and distant horizon where ocean and sky meet. The Southern Highlands lie chiefly to the south of the route from Dunkeld to Oban, by Loch Tay. This district embraces Stirling, Perth, and Dunkeld, with their immediate surroundings, including the Pass of Killiecrankie, with the famous lake scenery of Loch Tay, the Trossachs, Loch Katrine, Loch Lomond and Loch Awe, and the river scenery of the Tay and Forth, all making up the richest and most beautiful of northern landscapes.

Scottish scenery, taken as a whole, is equal to any lake scenery in the world. In none have we witnessed greater beauty than in our Highland "Lochs" When seen in their best lights, with their wooded islands, the infinitely varied curves of their shore line, the precipices streaked with white waterfalls, the wild copse-wood, and the mountains piled over all, they are unsurpassed, presenting as they do a .constant variety of outline and colour—some clothed with grass to their summits, others bare from the *débris* at their base up to their tortuous seams and jagged peaks. Here are broad glens and winding green straths, with moorlands rolling away; and there are streams innumerable, in little glens full of

LOCH EARN.

crystal pools and shadowed by ferns and primroses and drooping moss—streams too, strong and full-flooded like the Tay, the Dee, the Don, the Spey, the Findhorn, and the Lochy, with their banks clothed with surpassing beauty. And then the sea lochs, worming their way into the heart of the hills, with endless bights and bays, pretty headlands, and winding nooks of loveliness; every loch made alive by the ebbing and flowing of the tide, and by the curling seas. There are again, the great glens pouring down their storm blasts from silent peaks and corries of nameless hills, which hold converse with the clouds and changeful mists. And what of the mountain tarns? None but those who have explored some portion of the Highlands can realise the number of those bright eyes, shining in beauty, too minute and numerous to be indicated on any map or in any guide book. What spots there are, too, of unknown beauty, with their framework of lichen-coloured peaks, and their great boulders, gnarled trees, masses of blooming heather, and lakelets, visited only by the wild deer. Then the sea, which contributes so largely to the scenery of the West Highlands, revealing itself in every possible form—sometimes in salt-water rivers, sometimes in calm winding highways between the islands, but most grandly when it spreads its vastness to the horizon, everywhere modifying and connecting the landscape of the earth with the scenery of cloudland and sky above.

To fully realise this vast variety of scenery, we have only to climb some central mountain in the West Highlands We must ascend the green slopes, pass along the sides of the burns, thread the pine wood, and front the precipices and " sevidans," till from the windy summit we scan the inland lakes and tarns, and gaze on the vast extent of hills and the ocean far away, in order to see how great is the variety of our Scottish Highland scenery.

In no other country, for example, do mountains rise from an expanse so vast. Where, save in the north, is there any scene like the Moor of Rannoch, with its bleakness, with its bleached boulders and deep cuts in its surface, as if through its flesh into its bone, all filling up a space of twenty miles, bounded by shadowy hills ?

We do not attempt here to describe our Lake Scenery. This has already been done with a spirit and power which belong to " Christopher North " alone. But beautiful as it is, it wants the bare, dark, savage grandeur of the Western peaks and passes ; it gives no hint of the loneliness of the great Western glens, or of the solemn power of the great seas that roar against the grim headlands, or pour their cataracts on the reefs and islands of the outer Hebrides. Compared with this stern and sombre outer world, the lakes are as calm lagoons reflecting the form of quiet beauty sleeping in the arms of strength.

There are periods when there is no scenery visible in the Highlands save that of cloud and mist. Were it not for these mists the scenery would be wanting in much that contributes to its beauty. We should miss the waterfalls and cascades, and that world of beauty which is visible along

LOCH TAY.

the course of every tiny mountain rivulet, and in every crevice of the huge boulders scattered at the base of the mountains. The beginning and the ending of days of rain and cloud and grey mist, so memorable in what they conceal from the traveller, are the precise times in which marvellous effects of light may be witnessed. How transparent is the atmosphere charged with moisture, before that moisture is condensed so as to produce the "rainy day." How distances

diminish—the opposite shores of the loch and the distant
mountain being brought nigh, and every cleft and rocky
precipice and bare scaur revealed with vivid clearness. The
sun strikes through wild glens, and lights up the bare wet
rocky sides with a silver sheen; and distant promontories
come into view, and the line where sky and ocean meet is
so clearly seen surrounding both, yet so far away. And
then, what a sight it is! when the rain has spent itself, and
the clouds, which have emptied themselves, are rolling up like
a scroll, and every hillside is streaked with foaming streams,
while the green pastures revive, and the trees, gleaming with
diamond crops, "clap their hands with joy." What can surpass
the effects of the thin mist which veils the precipices, or wreathes
itself around them, then vanishes in light eddying vapour
from their summits, until lost in the intense and infinite
depths of azure. Can anything surpass the exquisite blues
and purples of the hills at such times, their indescribable
softness of outline, and impalpable film of misty light which
is cast over sea and land? And who can forget the effect
produced on the northern landscape when the clouds group
themselves in towering masses, while far above light fleecy
streaks break the expanse of the summer sky with the
glorious vista along the mountains, as range after range dis-
closes itself, until lost in distant peaks "that mingle with
the sky?"

Where can there be seen more glorious effects from colour
than on a clear day at morning or evening, when the rising
or the setting sun lights up the woods, with the arn and
birch and wild cherry, robed in orange and gold or bright
crimson, mingled with the dark pines and firs; and when
it fires the gorgeous purple heather of the mountains, and
brightens the masses of yellow fern?

And to the charms which these scenes possess in themselves must be added the fascination with which in most

minds they have been invested by the pen of the "Northern Magician." We were forcibly impressed with this when visiting the Trossachs for the first time. One old High- lander spoke to us frankly of the changes which had taken

LOCH TUMMEL

place in his day. "I and my father," he said, "used to guide the few travellers who came here up Ben Lomond. But no one will take my road now. And that is very curious, because it is the best! But the fact is," he added, with a peculiar smile; "more men are fools than I once believed! And what have you of it now but this—that a Lowlander—one of the name of Scott, or Sir Walter Scott, who knew nothing about the country—wrote a heap of lies on the Trossachs. I do assure you he told stories that neither I nor my father ever heard about this person and that who never lived here —about an *Eelen* and a FitzJames, and trash of that sort. Of course, ignorant Sassenachs take all that for gospel, and make new roads and build new hotels, and get new boats, and even steamboats and new guides, who laugh at the tourists and get their money. And so, you see, no one comes my old way to Ben Lomond now. But och! it's a sad sight, most lamentable, to see decent folk believing lies, lies, nothing but lies."

We write these notes among the " Braes of Lochaber." The scenery around exhibits all that is characteristic of the Western Highlands Let us suppose ourselves seated on a green headland, rising a few hundred feet above the sea level. In itself this elevation is remarkable for nothing more than the greenest grass; consequently, in the estimation of the shepherd, it is one of the "best places for ⌐wintering sheep"; and it is the more fitted for such a purpose owing to its being broken up by innumerable hollows and dykes of trap which afford shelter to the sheep from every wind. Moreover, the snow seldom lies here, as it is speedily thawed by the breath of the temperate sea. It has its own secluded spots of Highland beauty, too, although these are seldom, if ever, visited by any save the solitary herdboy. In these nooks nature, as if rejoicing in the undisturbed contemplation of her own grace and loveliness, lavishly grows her wild flowers and spreads out her drooping ferns. Nay, she seems unconsciously to adorn herself with tufts of primroses, bluebells, and heather, and slily retires into little recesses, to enter which one has to put aside the branches of mountain ash clothed with bunches of coral fruit, as well as the weeping birch and hazel, in order to get a glimpse of the rivulet that *whishes* between banks glorious with green mosses, lichens, ferns, honeysuckle, and wild roses. In the spring such recesses are a very home of love for piping birds.

Lifting our eyes and looking round, how thoroughly Highland the whole scene is, and how distinguished from every other of its characteristic features! Our promontory forms

the one side of the entrance to a salt-water beach, Loch Leven,
a branch of the great sea-river of Loch Linnhe, which flows
northward from Oban to the Caledonian Canal, and the hollow
of whose waters is continued in the line of the Great
Caledonian Valley, with its fresh-water lakes. Looking eastward, we are struck by the wonderful beauty of Loch Linnhe
itself. On the southern shore lies the green Ardshiel—one
of the homes of the Episcopalian and Jacobite families of
the Stewarts of Appin, who were ever faithful to their Church
and Prince "Charlie." Above and beyond Ardshiel is a
mountain, green to its rounded summit with fine strips of
native wood dotting its surface, forming beautiful curves,
and out of which, here and there, flash the cascades of rivulets

PASS OF KILLIECRANKIE.

that sweep downwards to the sea. Higher still, and beyond,
is a bare sharp ridge without a blade of grass. On the
opposite, or southern, side of Loch Leven, are upraised
beeches, with flats of fine alluvial soil, stretching out to the

shore, and backed by limestone hills of richest green, at the base of which little scattered white cottages nestle snugly. The winding shores sweep into sandy bays, which reflect white marble rocks, gleaming through trees.

But *the* grand and commanding object at the head of Loch Leven is Glencoe. Its precipices rise like a huge dark wall. Tremendous buttresses from base to summit disengage themselves from their surface, and separated from each other by depths such as might have been cut and cloven by Thor's great hammer, wielded in stormy passion. The mountain is scored across by deep lines as though they marked the successive floods of molten rook poured out by volcanic forces. Nothing can be more utterly sombre, sad, and desolate than this Glencoe. We have watched it in its every mood—sometimes when it seemed to sleep like a wearied giant, wrapped in the sun-mist; sometimes when it began to arrest the western clouds, until, as if overcome by their stifling power, they covered it with impenetrable masses black as night; or, again, when slowly and solemnly it unveiled itself after the storm, and the sun crept up to it, after visiting the green fields and the trees below, until at last it scattered the clouds from the dark precipices and sent the mists flying —not fiercely, but kindly, not hastily, but slowly—in white smoke up the glens, tinging with auroral light the dark ridge as they streamed over it; while the infinite sky appeared without a cloud over all, and as if supported by the mighty pillars of the glen.

Let us refer to the impressions made by another scene by a writer who is well acquainted with Highland scenery, and who views it not only through feelings "unborrowed from the eye," but with the eye itself, informed and guided by a deep and exact knowledge of the geological structure of the country, which has moulded the outward forms on which fancy and imagination act and are acted upon. Professor Geikie gives this description of a scene in Sutherlandshire :—"You may stand on one of its higher eminences and look over a dreary expanse of verdureless rock, grey, cold, and bare, protruding from the heather in endless rounded crags and knolls, and dotted over with tarns and lochans, which, by their stillness, heighten the loneliness and solitude of the scene. Acres of sombre peat-moss mark the site of former lakes, and their dinginess and desolation form no incon-

GLEN LYON.

spicuous feature in the landscape. Few contrasts of scenery in the Highlands, when once beheld, are likely to be better remembered than that between the cold grey hue and monotonous undulations of this ancient gneiss, and the colour and form of the sandstone mountains that rise along its inner margin. These heights are among the noblest in the whole Highlands. They consist of red Cambrian sandstone lying on the upturned edges of the gneiss, and with their strata so little inclined that these can be traced by the eye on long horizontal bars on the sides of the steeper declivities. Viewed from the sea, the gneiss belt runs in a line of bare rough hills and low headlands, among which, save here and there along a larger water-course, or on a straggling patch of gravelly soil, one looks in vain for tree or field or patch of green to relieve the sterility of these lonely shores. Behind rise the sandstone mountains in a line of irregular but stately pyramids, their nearly level strata running along the hillsides like lines of masonry. Here and there the hand of time has rent them into deep rifts, from which long mounds of rubbish are rolled into the plains below, as stones are loosened from the shivered walls of an ancient battlement. Down their sides, which have sometimes well-nigh the steepness of a wall, vegetation finds but scanty room along the projecting ledges of the sandstone beds, where the heath and grass and wild flowers cluster over the rock in straggling lines and tufts of green. And yet, though nearly as bare as the gneiss below them, these lofty mountains are far from presenting the same aspect of barrenness. The prevailing colour of their component strata gives them a warm red hue which, even at noon, contrasts strongly with the grey of the platform of older rock. But it is at the close of day that the contrast is seen at its height. For then, when the sun is dipping beneath the distant Hebrides, and the shadows of night have already crept over the lower grounds, the gneiss, far as we can trace its corrugated outlines, is steeped in a cold blue tint, that passes away in the distance into the grey haze of the evening, while the sandstone mountains, towering proudly out of the gathering twilight, catch on their giant sides the full flush of sunset. Their own warm hue is thus heightened by the mingling crimson and gold of the western sky, and their summits, wreathed perhaps with rosy mist, glow again, as if they were parts, not of the earth, but of the heaven above them.

Watching their varying colours and the changes which the shifting light seems to work upon their strange forms, one might almost be tempted to believe that they are not

GLEN OGLE.

mountains at all, but pyramids and lines of battlement—the work perhaps of some primeval Titan, who once held sway in the north."

But there is yet another characteristic of Highland scenery: that which is created by our associations with the people of the land and their past history. There can be no doubt that the feelings with which we view any landscape, and the impressions made upon us by it, are to some extent a reflection of the light in which it has been already invested by the imagination. Ranges of hills can be found without number, whose outlines are finer and whose natural features are far more striking than those of the mountains that encircle Rome, or those that look down on Athens. Nothing can be more bare and desolate than the sober hills of Palestine. Yet how powerful is the mental influence which all these exercise. They lead captive every thought. They are too dear to be coldly criticised. We love, admire and are silent.

The power of association in affecting our appreciation of a Highland landscape has been very eloquently described in one of Lord Jeffrey's Essays. "Here," he says, alluding to Highland landscape, "we have lofty mountains, and rocky and lonely recesses, tufted woods hung over with precipices, lakes intersected with castled promontories, ample solitudes, of unploughed and untrodden valleys, nameless and gigantic ruins, and mountain echoes repeating the scream of the eagle, and the roar of the cataract. This, too, is beautiful; and, to those who can interpret the language it speaks, far more beautiful than the prosperous scene with which we have contrasted it Yet, lonely as it is, it is to the recollection of man and the suggestion of human feeling that its beauty also is owing. The mere forms and colours that compose its visible appearance are no more capable of exciting any emotion in the mind than the forms and colour of a Turkey carpet. It is sympathy with the present or the past, of the *imaginary* inhabitants of such a region, that alone gives it either interest or beauty; and the delight of those who behold it, will always be found to be in exact proportion to the force of their imaginations, and the warmth of their social affections. The leading impressions here, are those of romantic seclusion and primeval simplicity; lovers sequestered in these blissful solitudes, "from towns and toils remote," and rustic poets and philosophers communing with nature, and at a distance from the low pursuits and selfish malignity of ordinary mortals; then there is the sublime impresssion of the Mighty Power which piled the massive cliffs upon each other, and rent the mountains asunder and scattered their

giant fragments at their base; and all the images connected
with the monuments of ancient magnificence and extinguished
hostility, the feuds and the combats, and the triumphs of its
wild and primitive inhabitants, contrasted with the stillness
and desolation of the scenes in which they lie interred; and
the romantic ideas attached to their ancient traditions, and
the peculiarities of the actual life of their descendants, their
wild and enthusiastic poetry, their gloomy superstitions,

LOCH LEVEN, ARGYLLSHIRE.

their attachment to their chiefs, the dangers and the hardships
and enjoyments of their lonely huntings and fishings, their
pastoral shielings on the mountains in summer, and the tales
and the sports that amuse the little groups that are frozen
into their vast and trackless valleys in the winter. Add to
all this, the traces of vast and obscure antiquity that are
impressed on the language and the habits of the people,
and on the cliffs and caves and gulfy torrents of the land;

and the solemn and touching reflection, perpetually recurring, of the weakness and insignificance of perishable man, whose generations thus pass away into oblivion with all their toils and ambition; while nature holds on her unvarying course, and pours out her streams, and renews her forests, with undecaying activity.